IOg

Ian gould.
NO RELATION TO
mwm PHILLIP

Castles

Medieval Castles and Cities

Text by
Wolfgang F. Schuerl

translated by
Francisca Garvie

Cassell
London

Frontispiece:
Wurzburg, Marienberg Castle: the Scherenberg
gate dating from 1482.

CASSELL LTD.
35 Red Lion Square, London WC1R 4SG
and at Sydney, Auckland, Toronto, Johannesburg,
an affiliate of
Macmillan Publishing Co., Inc.,
New York

English translation © Arnoldo Mondadori Company Ltd.
© 1969 by Kodansha Ltd., Tokyo for the illustrations;
copyright © 1977 by Hasso Ebeling Verlag, Luxembourg
for the text.

First published in Great Britain 1978

ISBN 0 304 30192 2

Filmset by Keyspools Ltd., Golborne, Lancashire.
Printed in Italy by Arnoldo Mondadori Editore, Verona.

Contents

Introduction

The history of the medieval stone castles and towns which we can still admire today in many places begins in the 10th century, the period when Europe finally took shape as a well-defined and unmistakable social and cultural entity.

No doubt fortified buildings have existed since the beginning of time and all over the world remains still provide evidence of man's constant sense of threat and inborn need for protection. Urban settlements fortified by walls appeared soon after the end of the last ice age (e.g. Jericho in Palestine whose origins date back to the ninth millennium B.C.) This was the beginning of a development which culminated in the splendid urban civilizations of ancient Greece and Rome. For us, however, it is the castles and towns of the Middle Ages which are especially significant, for they serve to illustrate the social and economic changes generated first by the isolated nobility and then spreading to middle class communities. It was a period of aggressive and belligerent conflicts which led from the 'natural' economy to the money economy, from feudal ties to the monarchic national state, from total spiritual and physical subjection to emperor, pope and God to self-determination. It is also the first period of European history in the narrower sense of the term.

For several millennia, Mediterranean culture had remained relatively homogenous and for a long time it was able to absorb new peoples attracted by the mild climate and the many flourishing civilizations. However, the appearance of the Germans and later of the Islamic Arabs brought far-reaching changes and gave rise to totally new traditions. A lengthy and complex process which intermingled elements from Antiquity, Christianity and Germanic culture produced the Europe which was to have an enduring influence on the entire period of more recent history. This Europe developed as a form of resistance to Rome, which had incarnated the idea of an all-embracing world empire, the Imperium, to the authority of which even the Germanic tribes had initially succumbed.

In the five hundred years between the fall of the Western Roman Empire in 476 and the beginning of the High Middle Ages, there were numerous attempts to reconcile the heritage of Antiquity, Christianity and new experiences. But no period, not even the Carolingian at the time of its greatest brilliance, managed to create the kind of consciousness capable of generating a new social structure of historical tradition.

The stone castles which appeared throughout Europe from the late 10th century – in place of the simple fortifications of earthworks and wood – are evidence of the development and consolidation of a new social order, feudalism. According to cautious estimates, some 10,000 castles were built in Germany alone during the Middle Ages, while in France the number is estimated at over 20,000 and in Spain some 2,500 castles still survive. Even smaller countries still have a substantial number of medieval fortifications, with Belgium, for instance, boasting more than 900.

The development of the town in the Middle Ages is equally spectacular. Germany had some 40 towns in the year 900, while at the beginning of the modern age there were approximately 3,000. While the Germanic tribes which had advanced into Roman territory during the migration of nations had been decidedly averse to towns, every third or fourth German was now a town dweller.

The architecture tells us much about the social and private lives of the inhabitants; on the other hand it is not comprehensible without a knowledge of the historical facts and of the daily life of medieval man. That is why this book, which merely attempts to provide an introduction to the medieval world, describes the history of medieval castles and towns against the background of the social developments of that age.

The Middle Ages, a term coined by the humanists to describe the transitional period between the decline of Antiquity and its rediscovery at the threshold of the modern period, is generally regarded as beginning with the migration of nations (375) or with the fall of the Western Roman Empire (476). Even during imperial Roman times the ground was being prepared in the ancient Mediterranean world for events which were to shape the history of this area for centuries to come. Diocletian (284–305, died 316) gave the Roman Empire a new constitution and an absolute monarch on the model of the eastern despots, and under Constantine the focal point of Roman policy shifted to the eastern Mediterranean. In 326 Constantine chose Byzantium on the Bosphorus as his new capital and called it Constantinople. After this, the opposition between East and West emerged ever more clearly. And with the death of Theodosius in 395, the Empire was split definitively. In 476 the last Western Roman Emperor, Romulus Augustulus, was deposed, and the discontented army of mercenaries, made up mainly of Germans, appointed the son of a German prince, Odoacer, its military king.

While the Eastern Roman Empire smoothly evolved into the Byzantine Empire which, as the heir to Greek and Roman Antiquity, was to achieve great political power and extraordinary splendour and wealth in the next thousand years, the former Western Roman territory saw the birth of one Germanic state after another, the most enduring of which was the Kingdom of the Franks under the Merovingians and Carolingians. These Germanic States round the western Mediterranean basin did not regard themselves, however, as the destroyers of the Roman Empire but as its successors. The defeated Roman population was superior to its Germanic victors in every area of economics, culture and politics. The reconquest of considerable areas of the former Western Roman Empire by the Eastern Roman Emperor Justinian in the sixth century must also have reinforced the impression that the old Roman Empire still survived without a break. Things did not change until the Lombard invasion of Italy in 568 and the Arab conquest of North Africa and Spain in the 7th and early 8th century, which finally destroyed the political unity of the Roman Empire and the economic and cultural unity of the Mediterranean.

Various factors played a part in the process of dissociation of Western Europe from Eastern Rome (Byzantium) which followed, and without doubt the most important of these was the Roman Church. As the representative of God on earth the Pope claimed supreme authority in the Christian Church. In view of the German threat, however, he had to secure the support of the Eastern Roman (Byzantine) emperor, which meant that *de facto* it was the Eastern Roman emperor who exercized most power in the political and religious sphere. Often he interfered in the religious affairs of Rome for political purposes. This is why the Roman Catholic Church was continuously seeking political independence and turned for help to the West, where it encouraged any political opposition to Byzantium.

By now the Arabs controlled three-quarters of the Mediterranean area – the central Near East, the North African coast and the Iberian peninsula – and had also obtained maritime control over the Mediterranean. Eastern Rome had lost much of its zone of influence and the Mediterranean was no longer 'mare nostrum' 'our sea', as the Romans had called it, but formed a divide between the Christian and the Islamic world.

In 751 a decisive step towards the creation of Europe was taken. The last Merovingian king, Childeric III, had been deposed in 743. Now, in 751, the major domo of the Franks, Pippin, was crowned in Soissons and anointed by the papal legate Boniface. Thus was founded the Carolingian dynasty, with the express approval of Pope Zacharias. But this did not wholly break the links between Byzantium and the Roman Church. Negotiations continued, although it is interesting to note that now a power that had emerged in the West, namely the Kingdom of the Franks, took the part of mediator between the two.

Charlemagne, son of Pippin, consolidated the links between Rome and the Kingdom of the Franks and at Christmas in the year 800 the West finally achieved complete independence from the East with the crowning of Charlemagne as 'Roman' emperor. (Here again we see the survival of idea of the heritage of Rome.) For the first time the Christian West now had a legitimate ruler – on the model of the emperor in Constantinople. Charlemagne, who ruled over most of the former Western Roman Empire, was a real sovereign, but he only received the formal official legitimization of his rule from the Roman pope who was the spiritual and religious head of Christianity. Here we already see a characteristic feature of European history, the principle of the separation of State and Church, which in Byzantium were united in the person of the emperor.

Charlemagne's three grandsons split his empire into three, however, and soon hordes of people attacked it from all sides: Normans, Saracens, Slavs and Hungarians. New fights and unrest broke out and for a time the new kingdoms of the west seemed doomed to an early demise. Now the various princes were demanding full independence too. But at the same time the repulsion of the intruders, who were of course everyone's enemy, inspired a new sense of fellowship. For instance Otto I finally defeated the Hungarians (955) after numerous internal troubles and thus achieved German national unity. On his second march to Italy in 962 Otto had himself crowned emperor and thus laid the foundations of the Holy Roman Empire of the German Nation, thereby showing that the German Empire saw itself as the successor to the Roman Empire. The German Empire (the fusion of the German kingdom with the Roman imperial dignity) shaped much of the history of Europe in the next centuries, until its extinction in the second half of the 13th century with the death of the Hohenstaufen King Frederick II.

Meanwhile the pope had once again consolidated his secular power which Charlemagne had restricted mainly to spiritual matters. But very soon a serious moral degeneration occurred and the papal power became a hapless tool in the hands of factions of the Roman nobility. The church reform movements and the gain in strength of the German emperor finally led to a battle for power between pope and emperor, both of whom claimed universal authority. The Italian policy of Otto I, who had gained dominion over the Kingdom of Lombardy and saw himself as Roman emperor called upon to be the protector of the church, created the political basis for a power conflict between pope and emperor. Otto's imperial church policy and the grant of landed property and privileges to the bishops, whose appointment was entirely in the hands of the emperor, were designed to prevent the fragmentation of the empire and to reinforce the powers of the German king vis à vis the princes; in fact, however, it led straight to the conflict of investiture which was seriously to weaken the emperorship.

Another factor which fanned this conflict was the reform movement that began in the 10th century in protest against the secularization of monastic life and the intervention of secular potentates. It began in the monastery of Cluny in Burgundy which was founded between 909 and 910. Later it spread to Lotharingia, South Germany, Rome and finally throughout Europe. This monastic reform movement soon gave rise to demands for the reformation of the church as a whole which was increasingly being faced with the problems of the buying and selling of church preferments (simony) and the marriage of priests. Originally the emperor had encouraged the reformed papacy which was emerging as a result. But very soon Rome tried to free itself from all imperial influence by denying the sacred nature of the kingship. Politically, the papacy could rely on its alliance with the Normans in southern Italy during this period (1059). Nevertheless, the differences between pope and emperor turned into an open quarrel on the subject of which of the two had authority to appoint bishops.

The dispute over the right of investiture began under Gregory VII, a former monk from Cluny. His goal was the full submission of the emperor's secular power to the pope's spiritual power. At the Roman synod of 1075 the pope forbade the investiture of bishops by laymen, i.e. by the king, even if he was crowned (Roman) emperor, under threat of excommunication. At the Imperial Diet of Worms (1076) the German bishops thereupon declared Gregory VII deposed because his election had not been valid. The pope's reply was to excommunicate Henry IV, whereupon the bishops and princes broke away from the emperor; in fact the princes decided that the emperor should be deposed unless the ban was lifted within the year and Henry repented a year later before the pope at Canossa. This dispute about the right of investiture did not come to an end until 1122 with the Concordat of Worms concluded by Henry V and Pope Callixtus II. Henceforth the king gave up the right of investiture with ring and staff (bestowal of the 'spiritualia' or spiritual powers) and confined himself to investiture with the sceptre before ordination. (In Italy and Burgundy this conferment of royal rights and Church property – 'temporalia' – did not occur until six months after ordination.) The Roman papacy thus attained its spiritual and temporal independence while the empire lost the dominance over the church which Eastern Rome and Charlemagne had had in the past. Henceforth European politics evolved between the two poles of emperor and pope. This was the end of the Ottonian imperial church system. The bishops who had been imperial officials now became vassals of the empire and finally, by the 'enfeoffment' with land, spiritual princes of the empire. A further consequence was the strengthening of the secular princes in Germany who had supported the pope, which meant a strengthening of feudalism.

There is another phenomenon which could not have occurred without this strengthening of the Church and the new more profound religious spirit, and one to which chivalry and the medieval towns owe much: the crusader movement (1096–1291). With the crusades the pope's prestige reached its zenith. They were provoked by the advance of the Seljuk Turks, who conquered Syria and Jerusalem and totally defeated the Byzantine army in 1071 at the Battle of Manzikert. In response to the appeal of the Byzantine emperor Alexius Comnenus, and fired by the idea of conquering Jerusalem, the Christian knights joined forces, forgetting all national differences. But the crusades must not be regarded only as a religious movement, for they were also warlike expeditions which opened up the northern Italian and southern French ports to trade with the East. Once it became apparent that the crusades had not achieved their declared aim of 'liberating' the holy places in the long term, the real result of the crusades proved to be an economic upswing and the emergence of a rich middle class in Europe.

The economic improvement which was largely due to foreign trade led to the founding of many new good trading sites. Unlike the existing towns which were mainly administrative centres, these new towns were commercial and were given special rights by their founders. The princes renounced their royal privileges in the hope of obtaining great revenue in the form of taxes, and the towns obtained their own municipal rights, relating to the market, trade, rents, police, defence, finance etc. With the gradual weakening of the emperor's central authority, they almost acquired the status of small independent states, like the imperial towns of Germany and the city-states of

Italy, which were fully independent. Often they joined into city leagues, which gave them great political power.

Europe's encounter with the East, and in particular with the highly-developed Byzantine and Arab art and scholarship, led to a general economic boom and promoted trade and the crafts; at the same time it inspired a more outward-looking attitude and raised the general cultural level. Until then, early medieval society had lived in a rather enclosed world, but now the contact and comparison with other cultures led to the development of a stronger national and cultural awareness in Europe.

Yet the unity of the Church, which had consolidated itself against the background of the crusades in the 12th and 13th centuries, now found itself faced with a threat which gave rise to much uncertainty and confusion: the heretic movements. These had emerged from sects which disputed the rights of the church to temporal authority and property following its growth in power, and called instead for simplicity and poverty. The two main groups were the Cathars, the 'pure' ones, and the Waldensians. The Cathars, or Albigensians after the southern French town of Albi, can be traced back to the Bulgarian sect of Bogumiles which was presumably originally Manichaean (Persia, third century A.D.). The Cathars taught a strict dualism between God and the principle of evil and rejected the sacraments of the Church. They rejected purgatory and requiem masses, military service and capital punishment. During the so-called Albigensian Wars (1209–1229), they were exterminated by the French king in extremely barbarous fashion at the behest of the pope. This brought to an end the Provençal troubadour culture and Languedoc, the centre of 'Catharism', was extensively destroyed. The Waldensians, founded by the Lyons merchant Peter Waldo, preached lay sermons against secular life and eventually repudiated the teachings of the Church.

These two movements formed part of a general, more or less radical, socio-religious current of thought which had sprung from the Cluniac reform movements and the Gregorian religious renewal. The Church, however, while consolidating its position, had to suppress the reform movements because they were a threat to its unity and newly-won power. The prime instrument for the suppression of heresy ('contrary opinion') was the Inquisition.

This was the source of the contradiction inherent in the fact that the Church increased its temporal power as a result of an increased consciousness of its spiritual tasks. In freeing itself from the authority of the emperor, from its secular ties, it in fact became entangled in secular matters and had to oppose precisely those attitudes which had once generated its own hostility to the emperorship.

The Church reform movement did, however, also produce a force which never abandoned the official Church view and yet tried to restrain the secularization of the Church: the mendicant orders. They adhered to the reforming principles of the 'Imitatio Christi', of imitating the life of Christ in poverty and humility. The Franciscan Friars Minor or Minorites followed Francis of Assisi and concentrated on awakening the piety of the people. The Dominician order was founded by Dominic of Caldruega in 1216 and aimed above all at combating heresy, which is why it also became the order of the Inquisition from 1231 on. The mendicant monks did not retire behind their monastery walls but mixed with the ordinary people as itinerant preachers and looked after the poor. The two mendicant orders had the greatest inflence on the development of the Church in the Middle Ages since they combined apostolic life with Catholic doctrine, active love with theological knowledge.

In the 13th and 14th centuries the two political powers which until then had been the greatest in Europe, emperorship and papacy, lost their pre-eminent position. The death of the Hohenstaufen emperor Frederick II in 1250 also meant the decline of the universal Western empire. Italy and Germany joined the other national states which had emerged as new political powers from the long dispute between emperor and pope. At first France assumed the leadership of Europe. The decline of imperial power also strengthened the princes in Germany and led to the creation of territorial states there.

Under Pope Boniface VIII (1294–1303) the papacy laid claim for the last time to total world authority. But the differences with the French king, Philip the Fair of France (Philip IV, 1285–1314), showed how anachronistic this political claim had come to be. In 1303 the unscrupulous and power-hungry pope was attacked and arrested in Anagni by Philip IV's chancellor; he died broken-hearted the same year. In time to come the Curia fell entirely under the influence of France. In 1309 Clement V, the first of a series of French popes, moved to Avignon. This brought the medieval papacy practically to an end. During its nearly seventy years of 'Babylonian' captivity in Avignon, the Church lost much of its authority because of corruption and nepotism.

This 'Babylonian captivity of the Church' was followed by the Great Schism (1378–1417). For now there were two popes, one in Rome and one in Avignon. Europe was split into two camps. This state of affairs was not resolved until the Council of Constance (1414–1418) and the election of Martin V in 1417. The Councils of Constance and Basel (1431–1449) were called to reform the Church and they healed the split. But they were not able to halt the progressive corruption of the Church, whose secularization was reflected clearly in the person of the corrupt and unscrupulous Pope Alexander VI (1491–1503). The decline of Church authority coincided with the emergence of many princely 'Land' and national churches. Even at the Council of Constance the importance of the reform movements outside the Church had become clear during the disputes with the Prague professor Johann Hus who was burned as a heretic in 1415. And in the Hussite wars (1419–1436) the political claims of national groups which had hitherto been oppressed, in this case the Czechs, were asserted clearly.

The dispute between the highest temporal and highest spiritual power, between emperor and pope, had a decisive influence on the medieval history of Europe. Although the emperor was defeated in this dispute, the foundations of Church authority were also undermined. In subsequent years England and France took over the leadership of Europe. After the conquest of Anglo-Saxon Britain by the Romanized Normans (Battle of Hastings, 1066), a very strong kingship had emerged in Britain whose Norman knights were the best warriors in Europe at the time. Under Henry II (1154–1189), the most important medieval English king, the so-called Angevin kingdom (after the ruling dynasty of Anjou then reigning in England) extended from the Scottish border to the Pyrenees and included more than half of France. In France, by contrast, the king's authority was weak at first and only gradually became an important political factor in the 12th century after a period of great feudal fragmentation. Typically, both countries gained their full national stability and strength in the warlike disputes in which they were embroiled with one another for over a hundred years.

The stronger France grew, the more tensions arose between the two countries. In the 14th century Philip IV 'the Fair' of France expanded his territory at the cost of the German Empire and successfully opposed the pope. Finally, problems of succession, and the French and English claims to Gascony, culminated in the Hundred Years War (1339–1453), which plunged France into great misery, aggravated by the spread of the Black Death throughout Europe (1347–1354). For a long time the changing military fortunes prevented any political settlement, until with the appearance of Joan of Arc (*c.* 1412–1431) the French national resistance became so strong that the English were driven out.

In England the Hundred Years War also produced a much stronger sense of nationhood, which led to a far-reaching break between the English and French cultures. The Wars of the Roses (1455–1485) between the houses of Lancaster and York temporarily destroyed the constitutional and legal system in England, although these events hardly affected civilian life. This was a period when trade and the crafts were flourishing. Once the two rivals to the throne had destroyed each other, there began with Henry VII the strong rule of the Tudor dynasty, which was to last until 1603.

In this way France and England achieved national unity by the late 15th century; both consolidated their centralised kingdoms, while Germany and Italy sank into territorial separatism.

In the Middle Ages the basic Roman idea of world authority had been incarnated in the papacy and the emperorship. But the struggle between these two supreme powers generated the idea of the autonomous national state and national self-determination. Until then a system of mutual trust between feudal lord and vassal had acted as the main factor of social cohesion in medieval society, but now the feudal state was gradually replaced by the bureaucratic state, in which the will of the ruler was carried out by officials who could be removed at any time.

This is the background to the splendid sacred architecture but also to the castles and towns and to the development of man amidst the problems of his time. The 'timeless' opposition between this world and the other world had always been a feature of the Church's lay teaching. But as knights and burgesses became aware of their historical roles, they consciously tried to understand themselves. The secular ruling class increasingly determined the image of man in that period. This picture now included and incorporated not only religion, piety and firm belief in the Church but also worldly values such as beauty, wealth, splendour, nature and art. Courtly love became the focus of the knight's thoughts. Earlier ages trained man to turn away from the world to asceticism and resignation; the new, independent world view brought with it a tension which could easily turn into tragic conflict.

The economic, social and cultural changes of the Middle Ages took place between the two poles of knighthood and middle classes, and brought about the overthrow of medieval feudalism. Men who lived in castles perched on remote hill-tops, or cut off from the surrounding country by moats, had been trained from childhood to carry arms and to fight for their lords on horseback. Their concept of honour and duty, of tournaments and courtly love, produced a new literary genre, courtly poetry. The knights defended the weak and fought the 'infidel'. During the crusades in particular they formed part of a convincing general European picture. The age of chivalry had its final flowering under Emperor Maximilian I (1493–1519), the 'last of the knights', who had to borrow the valuables for his splendid feasts from the Augsburg Fugger family to whom he had pawned them because he was always short of money.

The rise of the middle classes took place in the emerging towns. Anyone who moved from the country into the town and was not recalled by his overlord within 'a year and a day' became a freeman. The saying 'town air liberates' aptly described the social function of the medieval towns. Their economic basis lay in trade and crafts. The achievements of the early middle classes in economics, law and general culture led to new state structures although this class did not obtain political leadership until the French Revolution in 1789.

Castles and Knights

The Knighthood

After the fall of the Western Roman Empire in 476, the Roman social structure gradually disintegrated, although individual German princes did attempt to maintain the Roman administrative system. The complete change of economic structure, however, brought the system of civil administration to an end. The Arab invasions from the 7th century on destroyed both the cultural unity and the economic uniformity of the Mediterranean, for the Roman money economy had been based on trade in that area, which also meant political control. Now the Mediterranean separated two contrasting worlds, the Islamic East and the Christian West. At the same time the political and economic emphasis shifted to the north so that the Frankish Merovingian kings, for instance, now ruled from Paris or Metz. The shift in the balance of power and the emergence of new zones of political influence disrupted the international trade which had been the foundation of the Roman economy.

In the early Middle Ages, the early Roman-German kingdoms, some of them in areas formerly administered by the Romans, had been based solely on a natural economy system. Now, however, wealth was derived not from trade and capital but from land ownership. This made the system of civil administration quite impossible, of course, since the officials could no longer be paid. What emerged instead was a feudal aristocracy. The king would reward the nobles for their services by granting them the use of royal domain. In return for this 'feudum' or 'beneficium', as the fief was called, the vassal (from Celto-Roman 'gwas', late Latin 'vassus' = servant), would swear fealty to his landlord, thus also assuring the king of the allegiance of his followers, which included forty days a year of military service. In the beginning the fief was granted on an individual basis and on the death of the lord or the vassal the land would revert to the crown, as it would if the vassal broke his oath of fealty. The feudal system became the determining feature of the social fabric of the Middle Ages although at a fairly early stage the conflict between the vassal's fealty and his economic interests was resolved in a favour of the latter. At the Council of Coulaines in 843 it was decided that the king could not revoke a benefice except for important reasons. The Capitular of Quierzy in 877 decreed that the fief should pass on to the heir. Soon the fief was regarded as hereditary and in addition the holder could in turn hand over part of his fief to his vassals as a mesne-fief. This practice tended to replace the original idea of investiture with crown land, and of the bond with the king. The roots of this new social structure lie in late Roman 'commendatio', under which a man entered the service of a lord as his vassal in return for 'victuals and vestment', and in the Germanic system of vassalage based on allegiance. In times of war, the German nobles by birth, a ruling class based on property and great achievements in battle which saw itself as descendants of the gods, would elect a king to whom they were then bound by personal allegiance. The earliest known German king and military leader was Ariovistus, leader of the Sueves, who was defeated by Caesar in 58 B.C., probably at Mühlhausen in Alsace. The German military kingdom became the Kingdom of the Franks and the German nobles became the Frankish service nobility (who received fiefs from the king in return for loyal service) which included the princely holders of the highest offices: chancellors, archbishops, bishops, abbots, earls, margraves and counts. Once these offices had become hereditary, the last three formed the class of the high nobility.

16

Krak des Chevaliers, Syria. Reconstruction

Originally the king alone had supreme legislative authority. He had the power of the ban, which included military expulsion and legal prohibition. At first the ban was a proclamation commanding or forbidding under threat or penalty. Later the ban also became the penalty itself and was a sentence of outlawry. In the Kingdom of the Franks, royal jurisdiction was exercized by the administrative officials appointed by the king in the royal administrative districts, the regions and the 'civitates' or towns. The king could also grant this power of jurisdiction, together with 'immunity' (Latin 'immunis' = exempt from public dues) to individual, particularly deserving landlords, usually bishops or abbots, for their fiefs. Under the Carolingians this system of immunity and jurisdiction became widespread so that the counts had no power of access or coercion in the area concerned. The lord was now

17

responsible for law and order in his own domain which was not subject to the royal privileges relating to taxation, military service or the administration of justice. He had full jurisdiction over both bondsmen and free men, as a result of which more and more free peasants and tenant farmers became bondsmen. The extension of the feudal system to encompass the authority of the state also fragmented the state's power and led to decentralization. The nobility became increasingly dominant, especially since it was able to extend its local power by its right to dispose of hereditary fiefs by buying or selling. The stronger the nobility grew, the weaker the power of the king became.

The Arab invasions of Europe brought decisive changes to the Frankish military system. In the seventh century the Arabs managed to conquer the whole of North Africa and in 711 General Tariq set off from Mount Jebel-at-Tariq (Gibraltar) for Spain and overran the kingdom of the Visigoths. The last king of the Visigoths, Roderick, elected one year before, fell in the crucial battle of Jerez de la Frontera. Very soon the whole of Spain fell under the Arab yoke, except for Asturia, a small Christian kingdom in the north. The Arabs even crossed the Pyrenees to enter the plains of southern France. In 720 they took Narbonne, then made lightning raids into Carcassone and Nîmes and advanced up the Rhône and Saône as far as Autun and Burgundy. They set Bordeaux alight and in 732 marched via Angoulême and Poitiers intending to plunder the rich town of Tours too. But about 20 km north-west of Poitiers they were met by Charles Martel, the major domo or royal steward of the Kingdom of the Franks, head of state and military leader, and his followers; and the Arabs were roundly defeated in a terrible battle (late October 732). This finally put a stop to the victorious advances of the Arabs which until then had seemed irresistible. Later the Arabs were even driven back over the Pyrenees. In 752 the Franks won back Nîmes, Maguelonne and Béziers and in 759 many of their Arab masters lost their lives at an uprising of the Visigothic inhabitants against them. This meant that Septimania, the area between the Pyrenees and the southern Rhône, was recovered from the Arab dominion.

In fact, the Battle of Tours and Poitiers had only halted an Arab raid, yet it also represented the first setback for the Moslems who had by now conquered large areas of Europe. The real reasons for the end of the Arab invasion of Europe probably lay in the difficulties of administering and supplying settlements in the rapidly expanding Islamic empire. But the Arabs continued to make incursions into Franconia as far as Provence, the Dauphiné and Switzerland (St Gall) up to the 10th century.

During the 8th century Arab invasions, Western Europe found itself confronted by an intrinsically superior military leadership. In fact it is surprising how far the Arab empire expanded during the short span of time from the death of Mohammed in 632. At that time the influence of Islam did not extend much beyond the Arab peninsula on the east coast of the Red Sea. By 711, a bare eighty years later, the Arabs controlled the area from the Pyrenees in the west to the Indus in the east, from the Caucasus and the Caspian Sea to Yemen. Until the Middle Ages, the Arab universal empire continued to represent a great challenge to Europe. The speed of attack and subtle military tactics impressed and troubled the Frankish military leadership. Finally, the Frankish army underwent a major change under Charles Martel who organized a third, mounted army of mercenaries to take the place of the German foot-soldiers. The Frankish army probably owed its military superiority, demonstrated in its victories over the Arabs and the Saxons, to the use of the coat of mail, which was clearly specific to the Franks, and of the sword. Both were much sought-after articles abroad, but as a rule it was forbidden to export them. Yet it only became possible to fight really

3 Sidon (now Saida), Lebanon. The very ancient harbour town, once the Phoenician capital and then taken over by various different peoples, was an episcopal see in early Christian times. The old crusader castle projecting out from the coast recalls the colourful history of the town during the crusades. After the First Crusade it was besieged by Baldwin I, King of Jerusalem, in 1107 and captured by the crusader knights in 1111. It was occupied by Saladin in 1187 but regained by the Christians in 1228. Twenty years later it was destroyed by the Mohammedans and rebuilt by St Louis in 1253. In 1260 Sidon was devastated by the Mongols and then it was conquered by the Mamelukes in the fateful year of 1291.

effectively with this equipment after the introduction of the stirrup, the saddle and the horseshoe in the early 9th century. The improved and more expensive armour, constant training in arms and continuous preparation for war meant that the armed horsemen had to be wealthy. That is why, in the Carolingian period, warriors were often granted Church land in order to ensure their subsistence, preparedness for war and allegiance to their lord. So the high nobility was now joined by a lesser nobility made up of knights who performed their military service on horseback. Most of them were bondsmen ('ministeriales') of the king and the big landlords and vassals of the crown; then there were sub-vassals and, in the beginning, adventurers too, provided they had enough money for their equipment. The enfeoffment of the lesser nobility gradually made them free, and the granting of special rights produced a new class of mercenary warriors, the knights. Accordingly a distinction is made between 'Herren' and 'Ritter' in Germany, lords and knights in England, 'barons' and 'chevaliers' in France, 'grandees' and 'hidalgos' in Spain.

Once the fief had generally become hereditary, the profession of knight tended to pass down from father to son. Without this, the knighthood could never have become a specific way of life and cultural form. The 'Bayeaux Tapestry' from the last third of the eleventh century already depicts the typical knight, seated on his charger, armed with sword and spear, wearing a long coat of chain mail (German 'harnasch'; 'halsberge' is that which hides all), a conical helmet and a large shield tapering to a point. Later the light and fragile spear gave way to the heavier lance. This armour was not cheap. A knight's horse cost from four to eight times the price of an ox in France. A coat of armour cost about 100 sous, the price of a medium-sized farm. A knight needed some 150 hectares of land to pay for his equipment and living expenses. That is why the actual knights' companies were numerically small. A medium-sized county of 200 to 250 communities could only supply 100 to 150 knights.

The special way of life of the knights, which culminated in the chivalric culture, also evolved in the 11th century. Only from that period on one can speak of the knighthood as a class. Before then, and before the crusades, anyone able to provide his own armour and horse who obeyed the royal call to arms was a mounted warrior, a cavalryman or a knight. The beginnings of the way of life, morals and culture which we define as chivalric only came with the influence of the Arabs in Spain and in particular in southern France. Just as this new class differed from other social groups, so too the knights' education and training assumed a form of its own. Once the noble-born boy was no longer a child (at age seven), he was taken into the charge of an outside knight or a taskmaster for his physical training. Reading and writing were frowned upon as 'priestly arts' which not even the perfect knight need bother about. More important to the noble-born boy was to learn hunting, especially falconry, and weaponry. In addition he had to master the social graces and the rules of jousting and acquire basic skills in poetry and song. From the age of fourteen he served as apprentice under another knight. Usually he was knighted (with the sword) when he was twenty-one, or later on a special occasion. Before being dubbed knight the apprentice had to take part in ceremonies of a quasi-religious character including fasting, confession, holy mass, and an oath of fealty to Church and king, swearing to honour women and protect widows, orphans and those in need of help. Then he had to gird the sword belt, the main insignia of the knighthood. Two knights would stand witness to his ancestry and blameless life. Finally he would be dubbed knight: the apprentice knelt between the witnesses, and a knight, usually of great repute, would strike him on his neck or once on each shoulder and on the neck with the flat side of the sword. This blow was in memory of the sufferings of

4 Salzburg, Austria. The fortress of Hochensalzburg was built in 1077 by Archbishop Gebhard, a follower of the pope during the investiture dispute. This castle, together with others, was intended to protect one of the main axis roads over the Alps. The complex was extended continually until the 17th century. View from the north.

Christ and was to be the last the knight would ever tolerate. Then the sword belt was buckled on, the helmet was placed on his head and he was handed his shield. A knight who infringed the knightly code of honour and law could forfeit his knighthood.

The education of girls was quite different. They too were often brought up outside the parental home (by the overlord or in a convent), but they were mainly trained in domestic duties and needlework. However, they also learned to read and write and were certainly better educated than the men. The convents of the time produced women of astonishing learning. An example is Herrad von Landsberg. the Abess of Hohenburg (now Odilienburg) who died in 1195 in Alsace. In her book, written in Latin, the 'Hortus deliciarium' or Garden of Delights, she collected and illustrated all

21

5

5 Salzburg, Austria. Hohensalzburg fortress. View from the north wall onto the 'Palas' and bell-tower.

6 Knights' armour and weapons in Eltz Castle in the Eifel valley.

6

that was known in theology, philosophy, astronomy, geography, history and art.

The special social position occupied by the knights was reflected in numerous privileges. Legally they were superior to the free men and could pass on their rank to any members of their family who were not professional soldiers. They were exempt from the payment of dues but could require the so-called knights' duty of their vassals, the peasants. If a knight was captured, he could not be tied; his word as a knight and the promise of ransom were sufficient security.

As a professional warrior the knight needed constant arms practice. That was the purpose of the tournaments which developed into the most splendid and magnificent ceremonies of knightly and courtly life. The tournament was a mock battle governed by strict rules which eventually spread throughout Europe, beginning in France where Godfrey of Preuilly had drawn up the first rules at the beginning of the eleventh century. For a long time only the nobility was entitled to take part, although later there were also civilian and even peasants' tournaments. Originally these tournaments were held only at court festivals, but at the height of the age of chivalry they became a permanent event. At that time there were four jousting associations in Germany, Swabian, Frankish, Bavarian and Rhenish, which were each split up into smaller groups. The princes of these Länder acted as heralds, announcing the events, organizing the lists, seeing to the servants and lodgings, checking the jousting skill of the participants before the event and making sure the tournament proceeded in orderly fashion. Victory at the tournament was considered as honourable as victory at battle although generally the weapons used were blunted. A distinction was made between various forms of fighting. In the 'buhurt' or tourney, bodies of knights armed only with lance and shield rushed at one another. In the joust two knights clashed at full gallop in order to unhorse each other. Barriers of wooden planks were erected across the lists between the jousters. Sometimes sharp weapons were also used, which could be a very bloody business, often ending with the combatants wounded, badly maimed or dead. For instance in 1241 at a tournament in Neuss near Cologne, sixty knights were killed.

The jousting arms consisted of the cuirass, a coat of armour mainly protecting the torso, the target, a shield with a hole on the right for the lance, and the lance itself, almost 3·70 m long and topped with a spike, for striking the opponent on the chest and unhorsing him. Sword, axe, club and pike were also used, the latter mainly for tourneys on foot. The knight was usually protected by greaves and a helmet decorated with a crest or, in Germany, a tall heavy helmet. The horses' flanks were protected by thick stray matting covered with a cloth bearing the knight's insignia.

Mock tournaments ('Schimpfrennen', from the Middle High German 'schimpf' = joke) were also organized, in which the opponents rode at each other protected only by straw helmets, carrying straw shields and wearing patchwork clothing. The site of the tournament was the outer courtyard of the castle between the outer wall and a second less fortified wall, and later the urban market place which was covered with a thick layer of straw. The knights fought within a rectangle fenced in with barriers, on one side of which were situated the platform for the referees and the stands for the female spectators, while the other three sides were reserved for the people. The end of the fight was decided by the referee or marshal of the tournament and the victor or victors received prizes which they often presented to the lady who had offered them signs of her favour (scarf, ribbons, etc). The prize originally consisted of simple gold chains and wreaths, weapons, embroideries or horses. In some cases rather odd prizes were offered. For instance at a tournament of the urban nobility of Magdeburg in 1229 the reward was a

7 Porchester Castle, Hampshire. The 12th-century keep, very typical of the time with its plain, rectangular form, was incorporated in the north-western corner of the old Roman fortress wall.

8 *Porchester Castle, Hampshire. The old Roman fortress wall dating from the 3rd century and between 6 and 10 ft thick, some 24 ft high, was originally surmounted by 20 towers. The Roman fortress was part of a defensive system designed to protect the Saxon coast ('litus Saxonicum'). In the 12th century the Normans built a castle within the walls of the Roman 'Portus Adurni' (fore-ground).*

beautiful young girl called Sophia. Eventually tournaments were forbidden by the spiritual and secular princes because of the number of accidents. In Germany the last imperial tournament was held in 1487, in France the last court tournament was held in 1559.

In the course of the centuries, knightly society acquired a 'courtly' character

9 *Carisbrooke Castle, Isle of Wight. This island off the south coast of England had been fortified since Roman times in view of the constant threat of attack and because, if taken, it could become a base for raids on the south coast. In the 11th century William FitzOsbern, a relative of William the Conqueror, built a Norman castle on the site of the old Roman fortifications.*

28

10 *Carisbrooke Castle, Isle of Wight. The 13th-century embrasure shows how skilful building techniques could provide a wider angle for shooting while still giving the archer sufficient protection.*

with the knight committed to the ideals of modesty, moderation and homage to women ('courtly love'), faithfulness and Christian charity. Here again the origins lie in France. This virtuous ideal reached a highpoint during the crusades and under the Hohenstaufen emperors found its highest expression in chivalric poetry, the 'Minnesang' and the courtly epic poems.

11 Pevensey Castle, Sussex. This castle, dating from the 11th to the 14th century, also incorporates remnants of an old Roman fortress wall. This is a view of the great gatehouse.

12 Pevensey Castle, Sussex. The medieval balistas shot stone bullets of this kind, which were in fact still used for the early firearms. These stone bullets, which were not always smoothed or rounded, could weigh up to twelve hundredweight.

The homage to women, or 'Minnedienst', is one of the most curious phenomena of chivalric culture. It reached its full flowering with the troubadours of Provence. Provençal language and literature has come down to us since the 10th century. This astonishing culture, largely forgotten today by the general public, was destroyed in the wars of the Albigensians (1208–29) against the southern French heretics, when the troubadours fled to the courts of Spain and the Sicilian Hohenstaufen court. The poetry of these knightly troubadours represents the earliest fully developed romanesque literature in existence. Its roots lie in Antiquity and in Arab literature beyond the Pyrenees, which also evolved a highly refined cult of woman; and it influenced the entire literature of Europe, in particular the poetry of courtly love, the Minnesang. The object of this love poetry was the glorification and transfiguration of the married woman, usually high-ranking, and to some extent it incorporated elements of the adoration of the Virgin.

The Provençal 'Art de trobar' means the art of finding or inventing verses. The 'verse finder' was the 'troubadour', the knightly poet, who was accompanied by a jongleur (minstrel), the 'joculator' or 'joglar'. Many and varied songs were heard in the Provence, merry and mournful, morning songs, evening serenades, dance songs and songs of war, shepherds' songs, legends and fables, and in addition the 'sirventes', songs of praise, mockery or accusation which aimed to influence public opinion.

In Arabic Spain and neighbouring southern France the fruitful influence of Arab culture on the newly emergent Europe was very marked. As early as 854 the Christian writer Alvaro complained that the Spanish Christians were neglecting their own literary traditions in favour of Arabic literature.

'My fellow Christians are delighted by the poems and romances of the Arabs; they study the works of Moslem theologians and philosophers, not in order to refute them but in order to acquire a correct and elegant Arab style. Where can one find a layman today who reads the Latin commentaries to the Holy Scriptures? Who still studies the Gospels, the prophets or the Apostles? Alas! the young Christians who excel most by their talents know of no literature, no language except the Arabic; greedily they read and study Arabic books; at enormous expense they collect whole libraries of these works and everywhere they sing the praises of Arab science. If anyone mentions Christian books they protest disdainfully that such works are unworthy of their attention. What a pity! The Christians have forgotten their own tongue and scarcely a man in a thousand can compose a letter to a friend in decent Latin! But when it is a question of writing in Arabic, what a number of people can express themselves in this language with the greatest elegance and compose verses which outshine even those of the Arabs in the correctness of their form.'

In 1064 an army made up of Norman, French and Burgundian warriors quite enexpectedly besieged the Arab border fortress of Barbastro south of the Pyrenees. In spite of giving their word of honour that the Arab garrison (of about 6000 men) would be allowed to depart freely if it surrendered, they massacred the Arabs in a dreadful blood bath and took the women as victors' booty. The papal legate brought 1000 Arab women to Italy, for Arab singers were highly valued at the European Christian courts for their harmonious music which had no equal in Europe, as we learn from contemporaries. One of the victors who returned with this musical booty was Duke William VIII of Aquitaine, Count of Poitiers and father of that famous first troubadour William IX of Aquitaine (1071–1127), a man more powerful than the king of France whose vassal he was, and ruler of the area from the Loire to the Pyrenees. He was a romantic figure and very much at odds with the church hierarchy, although he had led a crusade to Constantinople in 1100. He was also excommunicated several times because of his wild private life. Eleven poems by him have been handed down, including one song of repentance and

13 Pevensey Castle, Sussex. As a rule the castle water supply came from draw-wells situated either in the courtyard or in a special well-house. At times the sinking of the well proved very arduous and the hilltop location of the castle could require a well over 300 ft deep. That is why castles situated very high up often had to content themselves with cisterns for collecting the rainwater from the roofs. Originally the draw-well of Pevensey Castle was enclosed by a stone wall 3 ft high and probably covered over. The water was drawn up by a bucket attached to a cable-winch.

33

five crude and frivolous love songs in which the woman is merely the object of man's lust. But in curious contrast to these earlier songs, the later poems show a more spiritual concept of woman and love; the woman becomes 'my mistress' to whom faithfulness and blind obedience are due.

There can be no real doubt that this kind of adoration of woman and love poetry was brought to southern France by the Arabs from Spain (the influence is even stronger in Italy, e.g. Francis of Assisi, Dante). This is confirmed by the successful infiltration of the end-rhyme in the 11th century, a pre-Islamic feature peculiar to Arab poetry.

Courtly love poetry, whose main German representatives were Reinmar von Hagenau, Heinrich von Morungen and Walther von der Vogelweide, glorifies the loved one, the 'Minne', with a strange mixture of idealized passion and physical desire; it is marked by the hopeless longing of the Minnesinger for the chosen high-ranking lady, the wife of his overlord. But these songs are not so much distillations of experience as social entertainments, an aesthetic play with form and ideal content, an expression in song of the systematic code of courtly love. In reality the service of woman may often have taken quite different form. At any rate certain parts of the texts and illustrations on drinking vessels show a different, more worldly and often rather crude view of love.

1190–1230 was the period of flowering of the love song and the courtly epic poem, the main form of courtly literature throughout Europe. The epic poem or 'chanson de geste' depicts an idealized knightly hero in an idealised society and incorporates elements from Celtic, Antique and Oriental legends. Besides the Antique models and the legends which grew up around Charlemagne and his paladins (knightly heroes, from the Latin 'palatium' or palace), the best-known of which is the legend of Roland's death in the valley of Roncesvalles during the wars with the Arabs in Spain, medieval courtly literature chiefly drew on the legends of King Arthur and his knights.

The adventures told in the ancient British legends of King Arthur, in which the Celtic traditions which had been suppressed by the Saxons and Angles survived, intermingle in the French and above all in the German versions with the mystic and spiritualistic Eastern legend of the Holy Grail, derived from the very ancient concept of paradise on earth. The Holy Grail (old Spanish 'gral', Provençal 'grazal' = vessel) is a mysterious object which can bring its possessor earthly and heavenly happiness. But men can find it only if they are endowed with a humble, pure spirit, great courage and self-denial. In French legend, the grail is an enormous jewel worked in the form of a vessel out of which Christ offered the bread at the Last Supper and in which Joseph of Arimathea collected the blood of Christ at the Crucifixion. The grail was kept in a legendary castle on the hill of Montsalvage (Munsalvaesche) and protected by a special order of knights. This is probably a fusion of the Arab alchemists' concept of the philosopher's stone with the Christian miracle of the salvation and also with ancient Celtic heroic tales. The literature that grew out of this poetic and mythical complex expressed the courtly social ideal of the Middle Ages and its knightly virtues: courage, justice, wisdom and moderation.

Courtly poetry spread from northern France (Chrétien de Troyes with his Arthurian poetry) to east of the Rhine: Hartmann von Aue ('Erec', 1190, 'Iwein', 1200), Wolfram von Eschenbach ('Parzival', c. 1204), Gottfried von Strassburg ('Tristan und Isolde', c. 1210), to give only a few German examples.

Knightly and courtly culture reached its first full flowering in southern France and then spread over northern France and Flanders to Germany. During the crusades the various influences and types fused into a uniform, general European style, the first important cultural style of the new Europe.

Only six years after the death of Mohammed, Palestine, which had recently been under Byzantine and Persian rule, was conquered by the Arabs (638). Even before this time a constant flow of Arabs had been immigrating into Syria and Palestine so that these areas were already arabicized. The Arab conquerors behaved generously towards the Christian, Syrian and Greek-speaking inhabitants. The Christian pilgrims, mainly from Western Europe, were allowed to visit the Holy Places freely, provided they carried no arms and paid a duty to the Arabs. The tensions between Mohammedans and Christians only arose with the advent of the Fatimids, followers of a fanatical Mohammedan sect. When the church of the Holy Sepulchre in Jerusalem was destroyed in 1009, the Christian West was outraged. Finally, with the conquest of the Holy Land by the Seljuk Turks after 1070, the situation became acute. A year later the Byzantine Emperor Alexius I Comnenus was decisively defeated at the battle of Manzikert in Armenia – decisively in that the Turks had now set foot in the formerly Christian Asia Minor.

The appalled reaction of the West had two main causes. Since the 10th century the Church reform movements (stemming from Cluny) had led to a more intense piety and given new impetus to the idea of a pilgrimage to the Holy Land. At the same time a new militant Christian attitude had developed which culminated in the concept of the Christian knight who fought against the 'infidel' in Holy Wars and thus obtained remission from his sins. This was linked to the development of the so-called Truce of God movement which emerged at the end of the 10th century and which aimed at abolishing the feuds between the knights and at creating solidarity among all Christians. In 1074 Pope Gregory VII had planned to advance into the Holy Land with an army of knights in order to free the Eastern Christians and the Holy Places from the Turks. But his plan had come to nought because of his dispute with the emperor, Henry IV. After the founding of the first sultanate (Rum) in Asia Minor, envoys of the Byzantine emperor Alexius I Comnenus appeared at the Synod of Piacenza in 1095 bringing Pope Urban II a message with a plea for help. The chronicler Bernold describes the scene as follows: 'A legation from the Emperor of Constantinople came to this Synod and implored the Lord Pope and all believing Christians to give help against the heathens in order to defend the Holy Church which had almost been destroyed by the heathens who had advanced as far as the walls of the town of Constantinople. The Pope called upon many people to give this aid and to promise on oath to go there with God's will and most loyally to assist the Emperor to combat the heathens.'

The same year Urban II called a synod in Clermont where on 27 November he delivered his famous speech on the crusades, which was greeted with rapture by the people and which a contemporary witness, Fulcher of Chartres, has handed down to us:

'Beloved brothers,

Impelled by the demands of this time, I, Urban, who wear the Papal crown by the grace of God, supreme priest of the whole world, have come to you, the servants of God, to bring our brethren in the East the much promised and urgently required aid as soon as possible. The Turks and Arabs have attacked them and have advanced into the territory of Romania as far as the part of the Mediterranean that is called the arm of St George; and while penetrating ever deeper into the land of these Christians they conquered them seven times in battle, killed and captured a great many of them, destroyed the churches and laid waste the land. Unless you oppose them at once, the faithful servants of God in the East will no longer be able to withstand their onslaught.

That is why I request and urge you, and it is not I but the Lord who requests and urges you as heralds of Christ, poor and rich alike, to make haste to drive this vulgar vermin from the area inhabited by your brethren and to bring

35

14 *Dover Castle, Kent. The castle with its keep built by Henry II is situated at an altitude of some 460 ft. It has massive walls up to 22 ft thick; the keep stands nearly 90 ft high and the draw-well is over 390 ft deep. This photograph was taken from the old Roman lighthouse ('pharos').*

15 *Dover Castle, Kent. The 12th-century stairway in the keep.*

speedy help to the worshippers of Christ. I speak to those present and will also make this known to those who are absent, but it is Christ who commands . . . If those who set off lose their life on the way, on land or at sea or in battle against the heathens, their sins will be forgiven them at that moment, this I grant according to the power of God vested in me . . .

Let those who were formerly accustomed to fight traitorously against believers in private feuds, now fight against the infidels and bring to a victorious conclusion the war which should have begun long since; let those who were robbers until now become soldiers . . . let those who were once mercenaries for vile wages now gain eternal reward; may those who wore themselves out to the detriment of both their body and their soul now strive for a double reward. What more can I add? On the one side there will be the miserable wretches, on the other the truly rich; on one side the enemies of God, on the other his friends. Commit yourselves without hesitation; let the warriors arrange their affairs and find the necessary funds to pay for their expenses; when the winter is over and spring comes, they will set off joyfully with the Lord as their guide.'

Thus spoke the Pope and at once all his listeners were filled with holy fervour and decided nothing could be more glorious; a great number of those present declared on the spot that they would set off and promised to persuade others who had not taken part in the meeting to follow them. Thousands joined the cry 'Deus lo volt' (It is God's will!). The watchword was 'Jerusalem' and the symbol a cross attached to the breast. The idea of the Holy War, of the armed liberation of the Holy Places in return for remission of sins, threw the whole of Europe into an ecstasy of enthusiasm and invested the knighthood with an aura of sanctity.

At this time the military situation was not unfavourable for the West. The Seljuks had been weakened by succession disputes and were locked in mortal battle with the Arab Fatimids in Egypt. Yet the first, disorganized horde of Christian adventurers under the leadership of Peter the Hermit of Amiens was annihilated by the Bulgarians and Seljuks in 1096. During the next 200 years an almost uninterrupted stream of knights, pilgrims, adventurers and ordinary folk flowed into the Holy Land, some of whom settled there while others returned to Europe. The classical division into seven crusades only refers to particularly outstanding expeditions; yet it may be worth describing them briefly here to give some idea of the enormous size of the movement in Europe.

The First Crusade (1096–99) was led almost exclusively by French knights. Neither Emperor Henry IV, who had been defeated in the investiture dispute and exiled, nor the French King Philip I, who had been excommunicated by the pope for adultery, took part. It was therefore directed by the papal legate Adhemar, bishop of Le Puy. The princes set off for Constantinople by various routes, to meet up there. Godfrey of Bouillon, Duke of Lower Lorraine and leader of the Lotharingians, Walloons, and Brabants, moved down the Danube with his brothers Eustace and Baldwin. Raymond, Count of Saint-Gilles, travelled through northern Italy and Dalmatia with the southern French army. Robert, Count of Flanders, and Robert, Count of Normandy and son of William the Conqueror, advanced through Italy to Apulia with the northern French and Norman knights and then travelled by ship from Bari to the Balkan to join up there with the southern Italian Normans under Bohemond of Tarent and his nephew Tancred who had tried only a few years earlier to conquer the Byzantine provinces of Epirus and Macedonia.

Even this First Crusade involved terrible persecutions of the Jews in German towns. In Mainz alone over 1000 Jews were slaughtered during the passage of the crusaders. Anti-semitism flourished along the crusader routes and cost thousands of lives, for crusading masses, turned into fanatics by the idea of

16   Dover Castle, Kent. The 12th-century 'Constable's Gate'. With its enclosing wall, now destroyed, Dover Castle was one of the earliest walled castles of Europe.

39

the Holy War, saw the Jews as the murderers of Christ.

When the crusaders arrived in Constantinople in 1097, the Byzantine emperor did not greet them with any great enthusiasm: the heroes from the West looked so very barbaric and greedy for power; also they were so numerous that they might well be a danger for his empire. The Normans under Bohemond, who had already taken up arms against him once, looked particularly dangerous. There were well-armed knights and a countless, unarmed, colourful throng of monks, pilgrims, women and children many of whom had sold house and home since they did not intend to return but wanted to settle in the East.

After lengthy negotiations the Byzantine emperor finally managed to persuade the crusaders to swear fealty and allegiance to him, which meant that all the areas conquered by them would fall under Byzantine rule. But few of the knights took this oath seriously; at least none was to adhere to it.

In May 1097 the army moved to Asia Minor, successfully besieged Nicaea, which surrendered to the Byzantine emperor, and at the battle of Dorylaeum defeated Sultan Kilidj Arslan of Iconium, who never again dared challenge the knights to open war. During their difficult march through the desert country they drove the Turks out of Asia Minor and founded the first

17, 18 Windsor Castle, Berkshire. This castle has been the traditional residence of the rulers of England since the days of William the Conqueror who is responsible for the original building. The building work finally came to an end under the rule of Henry II. The Norman kings were well aware of the strategic advantages of its good location on a steep slope of the southern bank of the Thames. Moreover, it was sufficiently distant from London to keep any attackers at bay. In subsequent centuries the castle was extended and enlarged. Its present layout dates back to a large extent to the reign of Edward III (1327–1377) who converted the castle into a royal residence. In the 19th century the castle was heavily restored in a romantically coloured medieval style. A number of English kings are buried here.

19

crusader states in Syria (Baldwin in Edessa, Bohemond in Antioch). It was only the threats of the more pious of the crusaders that persuaded the princes to abandon the idea of annexing territory for the time being and to set off for Jerusalem, the real goal of the crusade. In January 1099 the army finally set off for Palestine, supported by a Genoese fleet. On 7 June the crusaders had their first glimpse of the Holy City which the Arab Fatimids had again taken from the Turks a year earlier. After a siege lasting five weeks, Jerusalem was stormed on 15 July 1099 after a terrible massacre of the inhabitants.

An unknown chronicler has written: 'In the town our pilgrims pursued and killed the Saracens as far as the Temple of Solomon where they had assembled and gave fierce battle to our men all day long until the whole temple was dripping with their blood. Finally, when they had forced the heathens to surrender, our men captured a great number of children and women in the temple and either killed them or let them live as they thought fit. A large group of heathens of both sexes had fled to the Temple of Solomon and Tancred and Gaston of Bearn had given them their banners as protection. Soon the crusaders were chasing through the town, collecting gold, silver horses and mules and plundering the houses, which were overflowing with riches. Then, happy and crying with joy, our people went to the tomb of our Saviour Jesus Christ and confessed their sins. Next morning they climbed onto the roof of the temple, attacked the Saracens, both men and women, and decapitated them with drawn sword. Some threw themselves from the temple.'

The Kingdom of Jerusalem was founded under Godfrey of Bouillon; he was succeeded on his death by his brother Baldwin, who assumed the title of king. The crusading states, the Kingdom of Jerusalem (1099–1187), the County of Tripoli (1102–1289), the County of Antioch (1098–1268) and the County of Edessa (1097–1146), were situated in the border area between Egypt and Mesopotamia, so that they controlled the most important trade routes. These states were constructed on the French model, as purely feudal states. The French barons built numerous castles (Ills. 2, 3) to protect their land and to ensure their independence; they always elected the current king of Jerusalem and could transfer their fief to others at will. Their rights were embodied in the

20

so-called 'Assises du royaume de Jérusalem'.

The way of life which now evolved at the eastern courts of the Franks (as all Europeans were called in the East) on the French model was colourful and brilliant. The knights with their lust for power and land found opportunity enough to embark on lucrative adventures and battles and nowhere were more splendid feasts or more charming women to be found than in the promised land and on the Syrian coast. The theologians quarrelled with the secular lords and both quarrelled among themselves. There were unending disputes about the religious situation of the country and its inhabitants, some of whom were non-Catholic – Greek, Armenian and Syrian Christians. A lively trade developed with the Italian sea towns whose fleets now penetrated into the eastern Mediterranean and founded trading colonies on the Near Eastern coast.

Those knights who remained in the Holy Land evolved a way of life and views of their own which often led to conflicts with the new armies of knights who came to Palestine. Fulcher of Chartres wrote with enthusiasm at the beginning of the 12th century: 'We who were Westerners have now become Eastern; he who was Roman or Frankish has here become Galilean or Palestinian; he who lived in Rheims or Chartres now regards himself as a citizen of Tyre or Antioch. Already, we have forgotten the places of our birth; already several among us no longer know them or at least no longer hear tell of them. Many of us already own houses and servants as a hereditary right in this land; some have married a woman who is not a compatriot but a Syrian, Armenian or even a baptized Saracen. Others again have surrounded themselves with a son-in-law, a daughter-in-law, a father-in-law or a stepson; others are surrounded by their nephews or even greatnephews; one may cultivate his vines, another his fields; they speak many different languages and yet they have already reached the stage where they understand each other. Various people are already fluent in the most diverse dialects and the most distant races are coming closer in trust to each other. It is rightly written that the lion and the ox eat out of the same trough. He who was once foreign is now indigenous; the pilgrim has become the citizen; day after day our relatives and nearest come here to us and give up what they own in the West. Those who were poor in their homeland, God has enriched here; he who had few pieces of gold has many bags full; to him who had only a farm of his own, God has given a town here. Why should he return to the West when he finds the East so favourable? God does not want those who have followed him with their cross to fall into need here. See, this is a great miracle which the whole world should admire.'

It is true that the Franks adopted many of the customs and usages of the Arabs. Baldwin of Edessa, King of Jerusalem, wore Arab dress, grew a long beard and ate from his carpet, crouched on the ground. Tancred of Antioch had himself portrayed on coins wearing Arab dress. An Arab invited to a Frankish house said with surprise: 'The knight offered an excellent table with extremely clean and tasty food. When he saw that I did not eat he said: "Eat, be of good courage! I never eat Frankish food but have Egyptian cooks and only eat what they prepare. Moreover, I never have pork in my house." I ate, but cautiously.'

The many castles (over 100) which soon sprang up throughout the country are among the most beautiful of the Middle Ages. They adopted the main elements of the European castles and supplemented them by flanking the walls and gates with towers and constructing outer courts, large storage rooms and cisterns – which the Arabs had probably taken over from the Byzantines. At any rate the 'Wall of Theodosius' (Constantinople) dating from the 5th century already displays important characteristics of later medieval walls in its system of two parallel walls (main and secondary wall)

44

Page 42:
19 The Tower of London: The White Tower, built by William the Conqueror in 1078 as a fortress, is one of the oldest rectangular keeps in England.

Pages 42–43:
20 The Tower of London. The Tower of London is situated on the northern bank of the Thames east of the city of London and is the oldest building in London. It was begun under William the Conqueror but most of the work was completed under Edward I (1273–1307). The ground plan of the very extensive castle precincts is an irregular pentagon. The castle is enclosed by walls and moats. The moat in the foreground of this illustration was dug out at the end of the 12th century during the reign of Richard the Lionheart and filled with water from the Thames. The double walls are protected by towers, including angle towers, and semi-circular bastions. At times the Tower of London was used as the royal residence of the English kings and also as a state prison (until 1820). The place of execution was originally situated in an open court inside the castle (until the mid-18th century). Today the Tower of London is used as an arsenal and barracks; there is a museum of weapons in the White Tower and the Wakefield Tower houses the treasure-vaults with the famous crown jewels.

protected by towers erected at regular intervals. The Frankish castles in the East are gigantic versions of European castles. They were built by individual barons or by the crusader orders at strategically important spots and gave military protection to the rulers of the country. Later, during the attacks of the Arabs and the Turks, they became the last bastions of the Europeans. One of the most impressive Palestinian castles dating from that time is Krak des Chevaliers (Ill. 2). The building was begun soon after 1110 but not completed until a century later. The Saracens besieged the fortress twelve times, but in vain, and it was only by a ruse that Sultan Baibars managed to take it in 1271. The interior of the massive and still apparently impregnable building is partly in Gothic style.

The Eastern castles differ from the Western ones in dimensions and in the decoration of the interior where the influence of Arab architecture is unmistakable, as we can see from the description of a castle room by the chronicler Wilbrand of Oldenburg: 'The floor is laid with mosaic; it represents water ruffled by a slight breeze and when one walks over it one is surprised not to leave traces of footsteps in the sand below. The walls of the room are covered in marble strips forming a panelling of great beauty. The vaulted ceiling is painted so that it seems as though one were looking up at the sky. In the middle of the room is a well of multicoloured and wonderfully polished marble. In the basin of the well there is a mosaic depicting a dragon which appears to be devouring several animals. A clear jet of water and the air entering through the open window give the room a delicious freshness.'

The sufferings of the Moslems under Christian rule are described by Ibn al Athir, an Arab chronicler (1160–1234): 'The lucky stars of Islam had sunk below the horizon and the sun of its destiny had hidden itself behind clouds. The banners of the infidel fluttered over the lands of the Moslems and the victories of the unjust overthrew the believers. At that time the Kingdom of the Franks extended from Mardin and Shaiketan in Mesopotamia to El Arish on the borders of Egypt; the only parts of Syria outside their domination were Aleppo, Edessa, Hama and Damascus. Their armies advanced in Diarbekir as far as Amida, in Dshiras as far as Ras-al-Ain and Nisibis. The Moslems of Rakka and Hauran found no protection against their cruelty. Except for Rahaba and the desert, they occupied all the roads to Damascus. Damascus itself had to hand over to them its Christian slaves and Aleppo had to pay them dues.'

While the Seljuks and Fatimids became reconciled in the following years, the crusader states grew increasingly weak as a result of internal strife. In 1144 and 1146 Edessa fell into the hands of the Turks, which led to the Second Crusade (1147–1149). Inspired by the fiery sermons of Bernard of Clairvaux, mystic, reformer and abbot of the Abbey of Clervaux which he had founded and which became the centre of the Cistercian Order, crusading fervour rose again in Europe. Under the leadership of the Hohenstaufen emperor Conrad III and of Louis VII of France, knights and unarmed hordes poured into and plundered the provinces of the Byzantine Empire. They were finally wiped out by the Turks in Asia Minor in bloody battles and only small remnants of the armies reached Antioch and Acre. Here the subsequent activities of the crusaders gradually became farcical. The crusade became more and more of a catastrophe as a result of the jealousy of the French king who accused his wife Eleanor of having an affair with her uncle, the prince of Antioch, which eventually led to their divorce. Besides other factional disputes there were also errors of strategy. The crusaders attacked Damascus, the only Mohammedan power which was well-disposed towards the Franks. But this senseless expedition failed and brought great losses, just like the attack against Ascalon. For inexplicable reasons the French blamed Byzantium and called for a crusade against the Byzantine Empire, although this empire was in fact

Pages 46–47:
21 Goodrich Castle, Herefordshire. View from the south onto the castle ruin surrounded by a moat and dating from the 12th to 14th centuries. It is striking with its buttresses, narrowing towards the top, which reinforce the towers. Buttress walls of this kind are very rare.

the last Eastern bastion against Islam. However, Conrad III, who had already set sail on 8 September 1148, opposed this scheme and the whole absurd enterprise came to nothing. The disastrous end of the Second Crusade was an overwhelming shock to Europe and greatly weakened the belief in the pope's infallibility as emissary of God.

This crusade was to have particularly dreadful, and at the time unforeseeable, consequences for France. The marital quarrels between the French king Louis VII and his wife Eleanor of Aquitaine ended in the dissolution of their marriage at the second Council of Beaugency in 1152. Eleanor married again, choosing Henry Plantagenet, son of Godfrey of Anjou and Matilda, widow of the German emperor Henry V and granddaughter of William the Conqueror who had defeated England at the Battle of Hastings. When the English king died without heir, Henry Plantagenet succeeded to the throne as Henry II. He was to become the most important English king of the Middle Ages and founder of the Anjou-Plantagenet dynasty (1154–1399). Henry inherited Anjou, Maine, Touraine and Normandy; his wife brought him the ancient Aquitaine territories of Poitou, Perigord, Limousin, Angoumois, Saintogne, Gascony, Auvergne and the county of Toulouse as dowry, so that almost the entire south-west of France came under English rule. Henry's domain was so vast as to make the power of the great French dynasty of Capetians look rather modest by comparison. This situation eventually led to the Hundred Years War between England and France (1139–1453) which was to lay France to waste and decimate it terribly.

To return to the crusades, in 1187 Sultan Saladin totally defeated the

22

22, 23 Pembroke Castle, Wales. This castle was built in c. 1200 by William Marshal, Earl of Pembroke, on the ledge of a cliff. The earliest part is the round keep in the inner courtyard originally covered by a cupola. It is some 80 ft high and has a diameter of 53 ft and serves as a typical example of the round keep. Ill. 23: View through a window of the gatehouse on the south-east corner of the castle wall. The masonry is worth noting here; in these early days very irregular stones of varying sizes were still used.

Pages 50–51:
24 Kenilworth Castle, Warwickshire. This castle was built in 1120 by Geoffrey de Clinton, Henry I's treasurer. Later it came into the possession of Simon de Montfort and was extended and converted by John of Gaunt and Robert Dudley, Earl of Leicester. The illustration shows the ruined great hall on the western side of the inner wall.

Christian armies at Hattin and took Jerusalem and the ports of Acre, Jaffa and Beirut. Unlike the crusader knights, however, he allowed the Christian inhabitants to depart unharmed. These conquests provoked the Third Crusade (1189–1192) under the leadership of the almost seventy-year-old Emperor Frederick I Barbarossa who had already taken part as a youth in the Second Crusade and who now set off for the Holy Land with an army of about 100,000 men. On the way, after a great victory at Iconium, he drowned in the Calycadnus (Saleph) on 10 June 1190 when, in spite of his companions' warnings, he decided to bathe in a cold mountain stream in the heat of June and probably suffered a heart attack. The death of Frederick Barbarossa was a heavy blow to the Third Crusade, which had been so successful until then and made a great impression in Asia Minor. An Armenian wrote in a letter to Sultan Saladin: 'Diverse peoples are in the German army; but harsh discipline and a truly terrible strictness holds them all together. If one of them commits a crime he is sacrificed like a sheep without much loss of words. Once a nobleman was accused of having gone too far in punishing a servant. At once the priests assembled and unanimously sentenced him to death; and although many interceded for him with the emperor, the man really was executed. They avoid sensual delights with the greatest caution; anyone who commits a sin in this respect is shunned by the others and sentenced to merciless punishment. All this out of sorrow for the Holy Sepulchre. It is a fact that many of them swear an oath not to wear any garment except the iron suit of armour for a long time, although their superiors are against this. Their tolerance of all kinds of hardship is really unique and incredible.'

Now, after the death of the emperor, many of them turned back. The son of Barbarossa, Duke Frederick of Swabia, led the remainder of the army on to Acre where he too died (1191) of a plague which continued to decimate the German army. But in the same year the English King Richard the Lionheart and Philip II Augustus, King of France, managed to take Acre. The English king also managed to keep the coast of Palestine free for the Italian trading republics; in addition he was assured by Saladin that the Christian pilgrims could once again go unharmed to Jerusalem.

The Fourth Crusade (1202–1204) was begun largely at the insistence of the doge of Venice, the aged Enrico Dandolo, and led to the conquest of Constantinople, thus satisfying Venice's interest in trade with the Levant and the Normans' lust for power. The pretext for the crusade was the appeal made by the exiled Prince Alexius on behalf of his father, Emperor Isaac II Angelus, who had been dethroned by his brother. Constantinople was taken by the crusaders twice, the second time it was sacked mercilessly and the damage done was far greater than during the later conquest of the town by the Turks (1453). A Russian passing through Constantinople writes of this in the 'Chronicle of Novgorod':

'The Franks entered the town on a Monday . . . the anniversary of St Basil, and made camp at a place where the emperor of the Greeks had stayed previously, in the Sanctuary of the Holy Saviour, where they spent the night. In the morning, when the sun had risen, they entered the church of Santa Sophia and after wrenching out the doors they destroyed the choir which was decorated with silver and with twelve silver columns where the priests stood. On the wall, they destroyed four altarpieces decorated with icons, and the Holy Altar and twelve crucifixes thereon with crosses chiselled like trees rising taller than a man. The altar walls inside the columns were made of beaten silver. They also stole an admirable table with jewels and a great gem, without knowing what damage they were doing. Then they looted forty chalices standing on the altar and silver candelabra, more than I could count, and silver vessels which the Greeks used for the highest ceremonies. They took the Book of the Gospels which was used to celebrate the Mysteries and the holy crosses with all the images of Christ and the altar-cloth and forty incense vessels of pure gold and all the gold and silver they could lay their hands on, including so many vessels of inestimable value, in the cupboards, on the walls and in the places where they were stored, that it would be impossible to count them. All that was just in the Church of Santa Sophia; they also looted the church of Santa Maria of Blachernes . . . and many other buildings inside and outside the walls, and more monasteries than we can count which were more beautiful than we can describe.'

This terrible looting and bloodbath lasted three days. Monasteries, churches and libraries were plundered and destroyed. Nuns were assaulted in their convents and wounded women and children lay dying in the streets. In the end, 'the great and beautiful town was laid to waste'.

In his 'Chronicle of the Crusades', one of the earliest surviving works of French prose, Geoffrey of Villehardouin said that 'never since the creation of the world' was so much booty collected in one town. It was 'so much that noone could assess it; gold and silver and vessels and precious stones and velvet and silk and garments of miniver and ermine and the rarest objects that can be found on earth.'

Constantinople was perhaps the richest town in the world at that time. For centuries the wealth of the Roman and Byzantine Empire and the Near East had been collected there. These valuable treasures were scattered throughout Europe; for instance, the bronze horses now decorating the church of St Mark in Venice came from the hippodrome in Constantinople. The insane internal disputes of the Christians, and their mad looting in the name of Christ, perhaps took their most grotesque form in the sharing out of relics during the following years when the Latin emperor was ruling in Constantinople (1204–1261).

Soissons received the veil of the Virgin, the heads of John the Baptist and St Stephen, the finger with which St Thomas had touched Christ. Amiens obtained a head which was also regarded as that of John the Baptist; Chartres was given the head of St Anne, by Louis de Blois, Pisa that of St John Chrysostomos, Cologne that of St Pantaleon, Amalfi the body of St Andrew. An English priest brought his relic of the True Cross to Bromholm in Norfolk where it was venerated as the Bromholm Cross. A beautifully worked Byzantine reliquary shrine which had been made for Constantine Porphyrogenitus as container for a piece of the True Cross reached Limburg an der Lahn where it remains today. A few years later the crown of thorns was pawned to the Venetians and then came into the hands of Louis IX. 'St Louis', as the French king was called after his canonization in 1297, built the Sainte Chapelle in Paris to house this relic.

The unfortunate outcome of the Fourth Crusade created some dismay in Europe too. In 1204 Pope Innocent III said sorrowfully:

'You assumed the task of liberating the Holy Land from the infidel. You were forbidden under threat of excommunication to attack any Christian country unless your passage was prohibited or you were not given support (and even then only provided this was not against the will of my legate). You had no claims or rights to the Greek lands. You were under the most solemn oath to Our Lord – and yet you totally ignored these vows. You drew your sword not against the infidel but against Christians. You did not conquer Jerusalem but Constantinople. You did not seek riches in heaven but earthly wealth. But what is even graver: you held nothing sacred – neither age nor sex. Before the eyes of the whole world you indulged in debauchery, adultery and prostitution. Not only did you assault married women and widows but even attacked women and virgins who had dedicated their life to Christ. You looted not only the treasures of the emperor and of the rich and poor burghers but even the Holy Places of the Churches of God. You broke into Holy

Places, stole the sacred altar objects – not even stopping at crucifixes – and robbed countless images and relics of the saints. Who then can be surprised that the defeated and shamed Greek Church should refuse all obedience to the Apostlic See? Who can be surprised that it now regards all Latins simply as traitors and henchmen of the Devil and considers them all villains?'

Emperor Frederick II set off on the Fifth Crusade from southern Italy. This crusade had been postponed for a year because of a severe plague whereupon the emperor had been summarily excommunicated by Pope Gregory IX, his mortal enemy. (Gregory's successor, Innocent IV, even had him declared deposed, which did not, however, prevent him from continuing to reign.) The much beset emperor complained as follows to his European colleagues, partly in order to gain their support: 'While We are making the greatest efforts and had hoped for much advice from the Roman church, We find that he whom We thought of as Our leader and guide has unexpectedly proved an opponent of this Our enterprise, and to such an extent that, dealing unjustly with Us, he has excommunicated Us and has openly opposed Our promises and pledges, on which We insist in the service of the Holy Land, and has done so not in a spirit of righteous fervour but arbitrarily . . . Moreover this Roman priest pays mercenaries with the money that he should give to those who are departing in the service of Christ, in order to injure Us in every way possible. But although this Roman high priest is going against Our wishes in all these matters and shamelessly trying to irritate Us in Our mildness, yet he in no way restrained Us from the service of Christ.

Know then with certainty that We have already set off from Brindisi towards Syria with Our galleys and vehicles, with a strong band of knights and a great number of warriors, and are journeying with all haste under a favourable wind and with Christ as Our guide.'

Although the pope had also threatened to occupy the Hohenstaufen kingdom of Sicily as soon as the emperor departed on the crusade, Frederick II set sail from Brindisi for Acre. This was to be the most peaceful of all the crusades. The emperor, who was an amateur of Arab culture and even spoke Arabic, was loved by the Arabs and after skilful negotiations in Acre managed to persuade Sultan Al-Kamil to return Jerusalem, together with Bethlehem and Nazareth and a corridor of land linking them to the remaining Christian areas on the coast. But by 1244 Jerusalem was lost again, this time for ever.

The Sixth (1248–1254) and the Seventh Crusade (1270) were totally unsuccessful. Both were led by King Louis IX, St Louis, who was captured in Egypt and only released on payment of a large ransom. Thereupon he remained in Syria for four years, fortifying the coastal towns and trying to put an end to the constant feuds between the barons. But after the king's return to France the barons again started endless disputes in which the trading settlements of the Italian sea towns now also joined. The 'War of Saint Sabas' (1256–1258) between the Venetian and the Genoese colony in Acre was increasingly self-destructive and permanently weakened the Christians' power of resistance in the coastal towns. In 1270 Louis IX sailed to Tunis where he and a large number of his warriors died of the plague.

Since the West had sent no help and the Eastern Frankish kingdoms had become too weak, it was easy for the Mamelukes of the Egyptian sultan to take them. In 1291 Acre, the last Christian stronghold, fell and the Christians had to abandon the cities of Tyre, Beirut and Sidon. Of the Christian towns in the East only the kingdoms of Armenia (till 1375) and Cyprus, which was taken over by Venice in 1498, managed to make a stand.

During the crusades, the fighting vanguard of the Christians was formed by the religious orders of knights, linking monkhood and knighthood; they could be regarded as the standing army of the Christians in Palestine. Towards the end of the 11th century, crusaders from Amalfi founded a

25 Kenilworth Castle, Warwickshire. The main buildings of the castle are grouped round the inner courtyard at the entrance of which stands the mighty Norman tower called 'Caesar's Tower'. Its walls are up to 12ft thick and its height is more than 80ft.

hospital in Jerusalem for poor and sick pilgrims. They were called the Hospitaller Knights of St John after the Church of St John which was situated beside the hospital. Later they took the three monks' vows of poverty, chastity and obedience and swore to serve at arms. The brotherhood was recognized by Pope Pascal II in 1113. They wore black robes with a white cross completed during the wars by a red tunic. In Palestine the Hospitallers built up a real state for their order with Margat as its capital where the grand master resided. After the Mameluke conquests the order withdrew first to Cyprus (1291) then to Rhodes (1310) and finally to Malta (1530–1798), hence the name Knights of Malta or simply Maltese Order. The Knights of Templar or Templars were founded by eight French knights in *c*. 1120. They derived their name from the Temple of Solomon in Jerusalem near which their house was situated. The rules of the order were drawn up by Bernard of Clairvaux. They were directly responsible to the pope and their dress consisted of white robes with a red cross. In 1291 this order also withdrew to Cyprus and eventually, at the urging of the French king, it was dissolved by Pope Clement V at the Council of Vienna.

The third order of knights was the Teutonic Order or Order of Teutonic Knights. Their robes were white with a black cross. Founded in Acre in 1198 on the model of the other orders by merchants from Bremen and Lübeck, they originally dedicated themselves mainly to tending the sick in Palestine. But the fourth grand master, Hermann of Salza, sought new tasks for his order in Europe. After settling temporarily in Siebenbürgen (where they founded Kronstadt) and then being expelled by Andrew II of Hungary in 1225, the order began to Christianize the Prussians at the request of the emperor and the pope. East of the river Weichsel they founded a German state of their order which did not become a secular duchy until 1525. The order protected the territory it had conquered with many castles and towns (Marienburg, Thorn, Königsberg). The seat of the grand master was transferred from Acre to Venice in 1291, to Marienburg in 1309 and back to Königsberg in 1457. The order was dissolved in Germany in 1809 by Napoleon, but it still exists in Austria. All three orders comprised knights, priests, and la brothers.

The aim of the crusader movement, the conquest of the Holy Land, had not been achieved in the long term. Instead Christian Byzantium had been so weakened by the Christian crusaders with the conquest of Constantinople during the Fourth Crusade that finally, 250 years later, it fell to the Turks who conquered the once great empire piece by piece. The position of the pope, the spiritual father or at least spokesman of the crusader movement, had suffered severely. For in fact the joint undertaking of the West had shown up the national interests of the individual states very clearly, marking the beginning of modern European development.

The idea of a Holy War gradually gave way to that of a peaceful mission. The Spanish Franciscan monk Ramon Lull wrote in 1298: 'I see the knights sail over the seas to the Holy Land imagining that they will win it back by force of arms; but in the end they are all exhausted without attaining their goal. I think these conquests can only be undertaken as you undertook them, Oh Lord, with your Apostles, that is to say by love, prayer and tears. So let the holy knights of religion set off, making the sign of the cross and imbued with the mercy of the Holy spirit and then preach to the infidel about the truths of the Passion of Christ.'

The crusades were the golden age of the knights. It was the time when the knightly ideals and ideas of courage, justice, wisdom and moderation were born, of loyalty to the master, not taking booty, interceding for the poor, the widows and the orphans. These were indeed noble ideals and they were reflected in magnificent literary works – but perhaps only there, for the wars were brutal and cruel, the crusaders' real motives were often greed, power and

26 Harlech Castle, Wales. This is a very good example of an 'Edwardian' castle (Edward I, 1272–1307), based on a regular ground plan. It was begun in 1283 and completed seven years later. The huge inner walls are surrounded by low outer walls, making it difficult to bring up siege-engines such as battering-rams and enabling the garrison to attack any assailants who had penetrated the outer wall from all sides without danger to the castle itself. At one time the sea came up to the castle cliff, so that supplies could be brought in that way – which was very important during the conquest of Wales by Edward I.

Harlech Castle, ground-plan
1   *Well*
2   *Granary*
3   *Postern*
4   *Chapel*
5   *Stair*
6   *Kitchen*

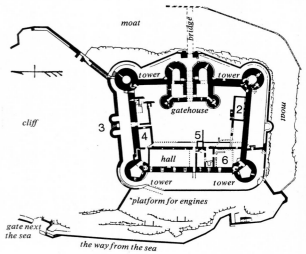

a fanatical hatred of anyone different, of unbelievers and heretics.

At the same time, the European knights were fighting the Arabs in Spain. So Pope Urban II sent the Spanish knights who had arrived to take part in the First Crusade back to Spain to combat the 'tyranny of the Saracens' there: 'Just as the knights of the other countries have decided unanimously to come to the aid of the Asian church and to liberate their brothers from the Saracen tyranny, so must you – and we urge you to do so – give support to your neighbouring church in persistent efforts to resist the onslaught of the Saracens! Anyone who falls in this battle for the love of God and his brothers will without a doubt find indulgence for his sins and everlasting life in accordance with the mercy and compassion of God. So any one of you who has decided to set off for Asia would do better to follow your pious impulse here. For there is no merit in freeing the Christians from the Saracens in one place and exposing them to Saracen tyranny and oppression in another. May the almighty God inspire brotherly love in your hearts and reward your courage with victory over your enemies.'

The reconquest ('reconquista') of Spain continued throughout the Middle Ages (in 1492 the last Arab ruler was driven out of Granada) and during its most successful phase it was closely linked to the crusader movement; it was the same battle against the infidel that was being conducted in the east. Often the two enterprises were combined: for instance German and English participants in the Second Crusade sailed to Portugal, took Lisbon by storm and presented it to the King of Portugal. The reform movement of Cluny also played a decisive part in the reconquest. Seventy-three monasteries of the new order were founded in Spain and became the spiritual and even military centres of the reconquest. Many of the Spanish bishops were monks who had come from Cluny, which had declared that the liberation of Spain from Arab dominion was also a Holy War. In 1063 Pope Alexander II promised remission of their sins to all who fought the infidel in Spain. The Castilian nobleman Rodrigo Diaz de Viva (1043–1099), called el Cid (in Arab, a master), became a legendary hero of the wars of liberation. Although he had fought for a time under the Arab Duke of Saragossa after quarrelling with King Alfonso VI of Leon for unknown reasons, it was thanks to him that the Arabs suffered their first decisive defeat in Spain when he occupied Valencia on his own initiative (1094). Poets and singers glorified his deeds, his courage and his great cunning, in countless ballads, legends and romances. With the continuing reconquest, new principalities emerged in Spain such as the county of Castile, which took its name from the many castles which were built in this open country in defence against the Arabs.

The 'reconquista' and the crusader movement had led to various contacts between a Europe which until then had been rather provincial and other, far superior cultures. There was the Byzantine Empire, the direct successor of Greek and Roman Antiquity, whose civilization must have had just as overwhelming an effect on the crusaders as the Late Roman culture had had on the German tribes in its time. Moreover, the contact with the Arabs, especially in Spain, was extremely fruitful for European development. Europe owes to the Arabs the heritage of the Ancient Greeks whose writings they systematically collected and translated at a time when reading and writing were disdained as 'priestly arts' in Europe; in addition, the Arabs were the founders of modern science, of experimental chemistry and physics, algebra and arithmetic, spherical trigonometry, geology and astronomy. They passed onto Europe countless inventions and improvements: the manufacture of paper, the compass, gunpowder, cannons, rockets, torpedoes and much else – some of which still bear the same name today, such as the term cipher, from the Arabic 'sifr' which stood for zero, another Arab concept.

Their medicine, deriving from observation of nature, led to astonishing cures

59

and discoveries (including circulation of the blood) at a time when European doctors still languished in the twilight zone between superstition and 'horse medicine'. In her informative book 'Allah's Sonne über dem Abendland' (1960), the German writer Sigrid Hunke tells the following story of an Arab

doctor who was called to attend to the crusaders: 'After only ten days Thabit stood before my uncle again. And we had believed he was healing Frankish wounds in the Lebanon! For my lord crusaders had damned little confidence in the medical art of their own people and preferred to have their rashes, colics and diarrhoeas treated by our doctors here in the Holy Land. And how right they were (may Allah curse them)! My uncle, the emir of Shizar, had done our Frankish neighbour at the castle of Munaitira the favour of lending him our clever Thabit for a while in order to do various cures for his sick friends. But Thabit was back from the Frankish garrison already.

'How ever did you heal the sick so quickly?' we asked him in surprise. 'They brought me a rider on whose leg an abscess had formed', replied the doctor, 'and a woman suffering from a hectic fever. I put a blistering plaster on the rider's leg. The abscess burst and healed well. I prescribed a special diet for the woman and improved her bodily health by giving her vegetal foods. Then a Frankish doctor joined us and said: "He does not know how to cure them". Thereupon he turned to the rider and asked him: "What would you prefer, to live with one leg or to die with two legs?" He answered, "To live with one leg." Then the Frankish doctor said, "Fetch me a strong rider with a sharp axe!" The rider with the axe came. I was still present. Now the doctor laid his patient's leg on a wooden block and ordered the rider: "Cut off his leg with a single blow of the axe!" The rider struck a blow while I was watching. But the leg was still not off. He struck again. Thereupon the marrow of the leg flowed out and the wretch died on the instant. Then the doctor examined the woman and said: "This woman has a devil in her head. Cut her hair off!" It was cut off and she ate the food of her compatriots again, garlic and mustard. The fever rose. The doctor said: "The devil has climbed into her head." With these words he grasped the shaving knife, made a diagonal cut in her head and pulled off the middle scalp laying bare the skull which he then rubbed with salt. The woman died on the hour. I asked the people, "Have you anything else for me to do?" They answered "No" and so I went, after learning things about their medical art which had hitherto been unknown to me."'

However, the more refined customs and more healthy way of life of the Arabs did gradually penetrate into Europe. At a time (tenth century), when the Arab town of Cordoba boasted a million inhabitants, 300 mosques, 60,000 palaces and large buildings, 1 university, 80 free schools and 300 public baths, an Arab traveller described the Kingdom of the Franks as follows: 'You have never seen anything dirtier than they are! They only clean and wash themselves once or twice a year in cold water. But they do not wash their clothes, once they have put them on, until they fall into rags.' Cordoba made a very deep impression on Christian Europe. The nun and poetess Hrotsvit (Roswitha) of Gandersheim wrote in the 10th century: 'In the western parts of the globe, there glowed a beautiful ornament, a venerable town, proud of its exceptional military power; a highly civilized town which was in the possession of the Spanish people, full of wealth and known by the famous name of Cordoba, excelling by its charms and famous far and wide for what it had to offer, overflowing in all seven streams of knowledge and famous too for its constant victories.'

It can be said that the heritage of Antiquity found in Byzantium and handed

Wildenstein Castle, Baden-Wurttemberg. This castle complex on the Danube dates from the first half of the sixteenth century. The main castle could only be reached via four drawbridges.

down by the Arabs, together with the Arabs' empirical scientific research, which laid the foundations of so many modern scientific disciplines, concluded that period in Europe which has sometimes been called the 'Dark Ages' and introduced the period which stands at the beginning of modern times. The Renaissance, the 'renascene' of Antiquity which produced a new art directed towards man and nature, and the beginning of scientific research, also marks the beginning of our 'modern' age. By setting off to drive out or even destroy the infidel, the knights were in fact taking the first step towards their own historical destruction; its contacts with 'the enemy' affected Europe so enduringly as to produce a radical social, economic and cultural transformation in which the feudal knight no longer had a place.

Construction, Siege and Defence of the Castle

By castle we usually mean a fortified building, or in the narrower sense the medieval fortified dwelling-place of a feudal lord. The medieval castle consists of at least one habitable, defensive building and a surrounding wall.
The wall surrounding the castle is the simplest and oldest form of stone fortification. It harks back to the prehistoric earth walls known to nearly all cultures and to Late Roman fortifications, and its purpose was to keep out attackers and protect defenders. Certain features of the masonry were adapted to the type of defence required, such as the battlements on top of the wall behind which the defenders could take shelter at any time. Embrasures are not found until after the introduction of the crossbow during the crusades; they eventually developed into the large crossbow embrasure in a protecting bay. The wall-walk behind the battlements was often built on a wide ledge which was either built of stone or reached by wooden structures. The wall-walk was not used only as a defence, however, but also served as a connecting passage between the various buildings; that is why it was usually roofed as protection against rain and snow. For this reason the wall-walk sometimes

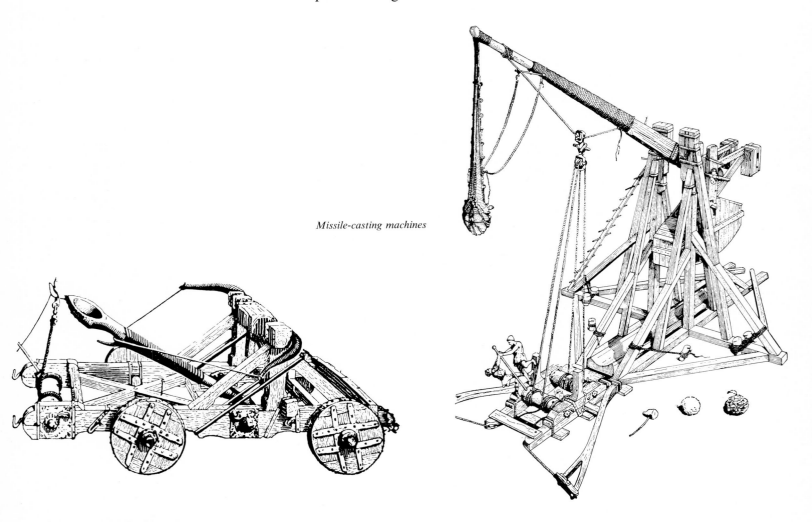

Missile-casting machines

ran round the towers and residential buildings – where the living accommodation was normally situated. The parapet often had pitch holes and machicolations (projecting gallery with openings in the floor) through which hot liquids (water, oil, tar, molten metal) could be poured on the assailants.

Some castles were built on hilltops, others on the flat land by a river or lake or surrounded by artificial moats. There was no fixed groundplan and the construction and aspect of the castles was determined instead by the nature of the terrain, the siege arms used and the military techniques employed.

In building a castle the main criterion was its defence against an army of besiegers. Right from the start, the basic principle of building castles was very simple: the castle must be situated as high up as possible. During a siege the garrison would defend itself by shooting arrows down from the high walls or throwing down stones or spears; the attackers used the same weapons, but were at a marked disadvantage because of the difference in altitude. That is why the principle of occupying the highest possible position remained the first criterion until the invention of gunpowder in the Late Middle Ages.

The development of castles was closely interwoven with that of weapons and siege techniques. The invention of new, more effective offensive weapons, siege engines and strategies had to be taken into account in the construction of a castle in order to ensure its defensive capability. Conversely, the construction of defensive castles led to the development of improved arms and strategies since this was the only hope of successfully besieging a stronger castle. After their decline in the early Middle Ages, around 1200 siege and defensive techniques again reached the standards of early Roman warfare, as we can see from the report of the Fourth Crusade chronicler, Geoffrey of Villehardouin, which deals with the siege of Constantinople (1203/4). In these days when an atomic war could very quickly annihilate the whole of mankind it is worth making a brief survey of the main weapons, war machines and offensive and defensive methods used in the Middle Ages in order to gain some idea of the kind of fighting around castles.

The most important medieval hand-to-hand weapons were the battleaxe, the lance (spear), the sword and shield, the bow and arrow, and the crossbow. The battleaxe was the Franks' main weapon and was still used by footsoldiers in the sixteenth century. It was designed for striking or throwing and had one cutting edge and a short handle. Among the Anglo-Saxons the blade was attached to a shaft 1·20–1·50 m long; they also had a short spear, mainly used by footsoldiers, while most of the knights used the sword, which was wide and rounded at the tip. The French sword was about 1 m long and straight, with two cutting edges.

The Norman knights of the eleventh century who are depicted on the 'Bayeaux Tapestry' were equipped with swords, long spears and large shields. As a rule the German shields were made of wickerwork covered in animal skin. They were about 2·50 m high and 60 cm thick. In the Frankish period a round shield armed with spikes was used. The Anglo-Saxon shield was also round or oval but was made of wood covered in leather. The Norman shield was rounded at the top and tapered to a point below. Later on, the wooden shields were covered with metal and decorated with armorial bearings.

The bow and arrow, known to almost all nations, developed into the crossbow after the crusades. The crossbow consisted of a shaft (wood, usually yew), the bow (steel or whalebone) and the bowstring which was spanned by a lever. The accuracy and penetration of this weapon was greater than that of any other small arms of the early Middle Ages. Its drawback was its considerable weight and the low firing frequency (about two arrows a minute). Yet the crossbow was probably the most important weapon in the

Caernarvon, ground-plan of castle and town

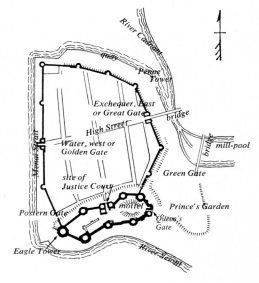

siege of castles. There were various types, some as long as 7 to 9 m (arbalest) which were placed on the platform of gates or towers or on wheels as field guns. Sometimes the groove was covered for shooting stone or lead balls. It was possible to shoot through a suit of armour at 250 paces with a ball-catch device.

In England there was also the longbow, measuring over 2 m in length; the arrow was 1 m long and feathered and had a range of 560 m. Unlike the crossbow, the longbow was light, easy to handle and quick to load; a practised archer could shoot up to twelve arrows a minute. In addition its range and penetration were greater than that of many crossbows. Both crossbow and longbow were still in use long after the development of firearms. There is a reference to a troop of English archers as late as 1627. Early medieval armour consisted of shield, helmet and the shirt of mail, a short bone or leather jerkin fitted with riveted links, chains or plates of metal or horn. At first the helmet did not have a nasal. Scenes on the Bayeaux Tapestry show that even the 11th-century Norman conquerors wore chain mail which was made of interwoven, riveted links and very difficult to manufacture until the invention of wire-drawing (after 1300). The helmets already have nasals here. The chain mail was still relatively light-weight but between the 13th and 14th centuries a shirt of mail made of both chains and metal plates came into use and by the 14th century the whole armour was made only of metal plates. In the 15th century this evolved into a very compact, heavy suit of armour in which it was scarcely possible to move. The horses also wore armour, consisting of the 'chanfron' for the head, the 'crinet' for the neck, the 'peytral' to protect the breast and the crupper over the hindquarters.

As regards long-range siege engines, a distinction is drawn between shooting and missile-casting arms. The mangonel and the balista, for instance, had a mechanism in which a strong, flexible wood was bent back by means of a system of ropes and pulleys; the projectiles were discharged at the target by the tension of the wood. The missile-throwing arms had fixed or moveable counterbalances or both. The trebuchet had a centrifugal lever, to the short arm of which was attached a heavy object; the long arm of the lever had a device to contain the missiles. The long arm was pulled down with the aid of ropes and a winch. When the rope was released the short arm with the weight shot the long arm upwards so that at its highest point the missile was released from the sling and hurled out. The missiles used were stones and beams of wood studded with nails, living captives and corpses, beehives and inflammable material such as the so-called 'Greek fire', a mixture of sulphur, tartar, pine resin, pitch, cooking salt, groundnut oil and olive oil.

The besiegers tried to ram the gates and weak parts of the wall with a battering ram, a pendulum beam with a metal head (usually in the form of a ram). The man-operated ram and its crew were protected from attack by a thick wooden roof (cat-house). Thus they could advance close up to the castle walls. The most powerful war engine used for hand-to-hand fighting was the moveable siege-tower. It was made of planks and beams and protected from fire by iron plates or untreated fresh skins. It ran on wheels so that once the ditches had been flattened it could be pushed close up to the castle wall. It had several storeys in which the warriors could hide and was so tall that it rose above the highest castle wall. Drawbridges were let down onto the wall and the assailants on the top platform attacked the defenders while the attackers in the lower storeys tried to break up the wall by various methods and to make a breach.

There are many written descriptions of the actual tactics of the castle siege dating from the beginning of the crusades until the introduction of firearms. A siege usually began with an attempt at ambush, that is a surprise attack and overpowering or bribing the guards. If this was not successful, and if the castle

32 *Conisborough Castle, Yorkshire. This castle, dating from the 12th to the 13th centuries, rises on a mound surrounded by a moat. Inside the enclosing wall, which takes up the whole hilltop, stands the massive three-storey keep (over 88 ft high, 52 ft in diameter), reinforced by six vast retaining walls (almost 9 ft thick). The stones are very carefully hewn here.*

could not be taken by storm either, the attack was usually confined to a blockade in which the besiegers surrounded the castle and cut if off from the outside world. We often think of the blockade as far more effective than it actually was. One reason was that the castle was seldom completely surrounded so that the inhabitants were still able to maintain some contact with the world outside and could obtain sufficient supplies. In addition, it was rather difficult to keep the medieval warrior in the field for longer than his period of service. Often the troops had to be released before the besieged inmates had been starved out. The situation changed substantially when the standing army of mercenaries was introduced. This made it possible to protract the blockade until the besiegers had an opportunity to construct counter-offensive stone castles.

The easiest way to penetrate a besieged castle was by scaling the walls. This was the procedure adopted in almost all medieval descriptions of sieges of castles. First came a concentrated shooting attack, then the wall was stormed with ladders, sometimes with double ladders equipped with four rows of rungs so that four warriors could climb at the same time. But this method was only successful if the preliminary shooting had caused great losses among the defenders and if the attackers had a considerably larger force of men.

Another method was to dig subterranean passages (sapping). Taking care that the defenders noticed nothing, tunnels were dug to the foundations of the main wall and towers. They were protected with wooden supports. Finally the wood was ignited so that the tunnels fell in and the walls and towers collapsed. Sometimes the passages even penetrated inside the castle. This method of secret entry into the castle through underground passages was used frequently in medieval sieges; this was how Philip II conquered Chateau Gaillard, which the English king Richard the Lionheart had built to defend Normandy, in 1203.

The siege and defence techniques became much more sophisticated during the crusades (1096–1291). The construction of the castles was also of necessity adapted to the development of more effective offensive weapons and siege engines. As a rule wet moats were now preferred to dry ditches; wider and deeper than before, they were designed to make it impossible to dig or fill up underground passages. The siege engines could not be advanced to the castle wall and gates until the ditches and a wall had been levelled. In an effort to reduce the danger of the fiery arrows, the wooden parts and the roofs were now painted with aqueous clay or covered in fresh animal skins. When the Greek Fire was used, the roofs of the buildings and towers were covered with lead plates and the angles of inclination were widened to give less hold to the balls of fire. The defenders also used a stone sling device called the small balista which could be lifted up onto the wall or tower once the wall-walks had been widened and the steep roofing of the towers was abandoned. In defence against stone-breaking engines like the battering-ram, walls were made increasingly thick and solid and strong parapets and towers were erected at specially dangerous points. Since the corners of the walls and towers were easy to destroy they were increasingly often rounded off. In addition, projecting towers were built on the encircling wall. This avoided any blind corners at ground level and made it possible to shoot from both sides at any besiegers who had advanced as far as the wall.

The decline of the medieval castle is linked to the development of firearms which were first used for castle sieges in the 14th century. The castles had managed to withstand arrows, crossbows and slingshot but the much heavier balls of stone or iron shot by the new artillery broke up even the strongest walls. Precisely because of their exposed situation the castles now represented an excellent target for the firearms whose accuracy was improving continually thanks to the flatter trajectory, greater power of penetration and longer range

70

of the projectiles. Although the castles were also armed with artillery and the walls were built lower and reinforced, by the 16th century this kind of fortification had finally lost all military importance. A new kind of fortress now emerged, built close to the ground and playing a different defensive role: fortified buildings were now erected at strategically important points not to protect a small family but to defend the entire land. The technical advances in metallurgy, such as forges and smelting ovens with bellows, and the changes in the military system produced a new kind of warfare so that the fortification builders increasingly became specialists, whose skills were also of growing interest to the towns. Many important architects, engineers and artists of the Renaissance were interested in questions of warfare, the best-known of whom are perhaps Leonardo da Vinci and Albrecht Dürer ('Unterricht zur Befestigung der Städte, Schlösser und Flecken' [Teaching on the fortification of towns, castles and areas], 1527). The main features of the castle were taken up again in the building of châteaux and palaces, beginning in France where a strong central kingdom had emerged early on, thus preventing the kind of feudal fragmentation that had occurred in Germany.

Development of European Castles

Since the birth of Christ at the very latest the German tribes had been familiar with fortified buildings, which the Roman historian Tacitus described in his 'Annales' in the first century A.D. But these castles were fundamentally

33 Conisborough Castle, Yorkshire. The masonry in the tower stairway is also formed of carefully worked stones.

different from the later, medieval ones. The early German refuge castles were used not as the habitation of one noble family but as places of refuge for fairly large numbers of people in times of great external danger. The walls were made of mounds of stone and earth held together by palisades of wattle

34 Warkworth Castle, Northumberland. This is one of the most strongly defended castles in the north of England. It was the seat of the earls of Northumberland and forms the backcloth to three scenes from Shakespeare's 'Henry IV'. The oldest parts date from

c. *1200: the south wall and gatehouse and 'Carrickfergus Tower', shown on this illustration, and the deep moat in front of it; the other three sides of the tower were protected by the steep incline of the cliff. The original drawbridge of the gatehouse has been replaced by a modern one.*

rammed in the ground. They were surrounded by wide ditches. The gates were inset so that any advancing assailants could be attacked from the flank. These castles were very large since they had to contain a considerable number of people seeking refuge. They also took advantage of the lie of the land. Unlike

73

the Roman castles of the time, the castles of refuge were situated in fairly inaccessible spots, on top of hills, in marshes, on islands in rivers, in bends of the river, and so on. It is probable that the Germans adopted a number of the techniques of Roman fortifications. There are scarcely any archaeological remains or revealing documents from the time after the fall of the Roman empire to give us more precise information. A new tradition developed from the surviving Roman castles and civil settlements: they became the sites of bishops' sees, as in Speyer, Trier, Augsburg, Cologne and Constance. According to a papal decree, the bishops' sees had to be located in towns. The historian Arbeo wrote in the 8th century that Regensburg was fortified with ashlar walls and was considered impregnable. At that time the town was the residence of the Bavarian dukes, which suggests that the model of the episcopal towns had now been adopted by the secular princes too. These secular building complexes include the royal courts of the Frankish and Carolingian period.

Charles Martel (the Hammer), the major domus (or mayor of the palace) of the Kingdom of the Franks, had been ruling since 737 without a king. He managed to reunite the fragmented kingdom of the Franks and to break the resistance of the northern German tribes. By an organized urban settlement scheme he colonized the Eastern Franks. Finally Charlemagne managed to incorporate the Saxons into the Kingdom of the Franks. This called for a comprehensive system of administration of the royal territories, and Frankish military and administrative centres, the royal manors, were now set up everywhere. They were planned on a rectangle like the Roman castles but were usually considerably smaller. They consisted of a redoubt and an earth rampart, the exterior of which comprised a wall about 1 metre high, a palisade of wattle enclosed by a ditch. Within the fortification stood wooden houses. In addition to their military and administrative purposes (tax, population census), these buildings were used for the visits of the royal court during the king's travels through his empire.

Even larger fortresses were built under Charlemagne on the model of the ancient palaces of Rome and Ravenna. The 'palatinates', whose name derived from the Palatine, the Roman hill on which the emperor's palaces were situated, were an expression of the enhanced power and dignity of the emperor at the same time as being new centres adapted to the changed political structure. There were famous imperial palaces in Ingelheim, Nimwegen and Aachen. They were the places where Charlemagne received foreign ambassadors and held imperial diets and synods. In addition to the upper hall ('aula regia') and the king's residential chambers, the palatinates included an administrative suite, a palatine chapel and often a palatine school, grouped round open interior courtyards. The Saxon emperors (919–1024) also adhered to the tradition of building palatinates (e.g. Goslar); but now the separate imperial dwelling became the central structure. The 'aula regia' on the model of the Roman assembly hall with an apse was now replaced by the throne room which is reminiscent more of the German royal halls described in the northern heroic sagas.

None of these palatinates were especially well fortified. Since the emperor moved from one place to another it was not very important if one palatinate temporarily fell into the hands of the enemy. This situation only changed with the growing rivalry between emperor and pope, when ambitious German princes could turn into dangerous enemies of the emperor. From the Ottonian period the imperial palatinates became strong defensive complexes and the emperors even rebuilt and reinforced existing palatinates. The Hohenstaufen imperial palatinates of Gelnhausen, Hagenau in the Alsace, Kaiserslautern, Wimpfen and Eger in Bohemia were still an expression of imperial power, but also of its sense of threat.

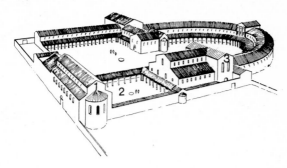

*Ingelheim, Palatinate of Charlemagne
Reconstruction*

1 Aula Regia
2 Atrium
3 Palatine Chapel

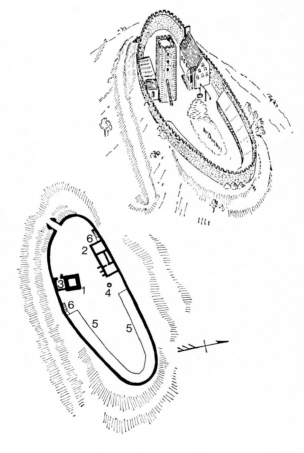

*(below)
Staufen, Breisgau
Reconstruction and ground-plan of the castle in
c. 1000)*

1 Bergfried (tower)
2 Palas (hall-range)
3 Chapel with cellar
4 Well
5 Living and domestic quarters
6 Wall-walk along the parapet

Beside the imperial palatinates, we now find the development of large princely castles. Originally it was the king's privilege alone to build castles. But the political unrest which shook Europe in the 10th century, the Hungarian raids which had decimated Germany, northern Italy and France from around 900 and the attacks of the Slavs and Normans, forced the high nobility to withdraw to secure castles around the turn of the millenium. It was then that the Guelfs built the castle of Ravensburg. Frederick of Büren moved to the castle of the Hohenstaufen, which became the dynastic name of the noble family. The Habsburgers also derive their name from their castle in Switzerland. This was also the period in which the word 'von' or 'de' (of) was first used to describe the nobility although until the end of the Middle Ages it still served purely to denote origin. Fortifications from earlier times were often the basis of the new castles. For instance the Honehstaufen Castle was built on the foundations of a Celtic fortress. The castles of the 'Ministeriales', the servile retainers of the king, and of the high nobility differ very little from the imperial castles.

A typical example of a castle of one of these princes, many of whom were opposing the emperor, is the citadel of Hohensalzburg (Ills. 4, 5) above the town of Salzburg which was begun in 1077 at the height of the investiture dispute by the prince bishop of Salzburg. The oldest part of the building is the 'Palas' or hall-range which is surrounded by its own wall. Soon after 1200 a wall enclosed the entire great crag on which it was built. In face of the Turksih threat the castle was converted into the strongest fortress of the Salzburg area in the mid-15th century while also being used as the bishop's residence. Between 1495 and 1519 Archbishop Leonard von Keutschach had new bastions added and the fortress continued to be converted and extended until the 17th century.

However, it was the lower nobility that was to return to a type of castle building which transformed the aspect of medieval castles in Germany.

The fortified, rectangular keep (French *donjon*) evolved in France; it consisted of a residential tower used for living, of substantial dimensions. The keep probably harks back to the very ancient fortifications and forts of the early Mediterranean civilizations, good examples of which are the round nuraghs in Sardinia. The Frankish nobles adopted this method of building, altering it according to their needs and technical skills. Originally the keep was built of wood, but by the 10th century a few of the towers were constructed of stone. The earliest surviving example is the keep of Langeais (Ill. 45) which Fulk Nerra built at the end of the 10th century. The Normans then developed this into the so-called motte-and-bailey castle which they introduced into England, Scotland, Ireland, Spain, Sicily, southern Italy and Palestine during their conquests. For wherever the Normans went, they dotted the land with numerous castles, partly as an expression of their agressive, belligerent nature and partly because of the need to dominate the occupied areas militarily. After the motte-and-bailey came the tall towers built on high ground. The Bayeaux Tapestry dating from the 11th century shows a typical tower castle and this kind of castle probably did not evolve much earlier than that date. It was brought to England with the Norman conquests.

Around 911 the Normans settled at the mouth of the river Seine. In the Treaty of Saint Clair-sur-Epte the king of the Franks, Charles III the Simple, recognized the Norman leader Rollo as his vassal and gave him that land in tenure. The Normans became converted to Christianity and adopted the language of their new homeland. Rollo's successors ruled the land, first as counts then as dukes and the area is called Normandy after them. This was the base from which they embarked on their conquests, the most momentous of which was probably the conquest of England in 1066. The Normans also

Two forms of motte and bailey. The conical mound of earth was enclosed by palisades and surrounded by a ditch. In front was the lower bailey which was similarly fortified and served as a place of refuge for the local people.

brought their castles to England where they were to assume a classical style which to some extent influenced the rest of Europe in turn.

Like the continent, England had built fortifications consisting of earth walls and ditches (earthworks) since prehistoric times, most of them taking advantage of the lie of the land, being on hill-tops, like Maiden Castle in Dorset and Old Sarum in Wiltshire.

Remains of city walls, houses and castles still survive from the period of Roman rule in England (1st to early 5th century A.D.) and they include many Roman fortresses built at the end of the 3rd century on the Saxon coast ('litus Saxonicum') between Brancaster in Norfolk and Portchester in Hampshire. Often the later medieval castles were built within Roman fortified walls, as in the case of Portchester Castle or Pevensey Castle in Sussex (Ill. 11).

Portchester Castle (Ill. 7, 8) had already been a mighty fortress under the Romans and was the base of the Roman fleet in England. The well-preserved external walls of the Roman castle are between 1·80 m and 3 m thick and about 8 m high. Twenty towers originally reinforced the wall which was enclosed by a trench.

In the middle of the 5th century, Jutes, Angles and Saxons landed in England and gradually conquered it. The Britons were driven back to the hilly west coast or fled to Armorica in Gaul, a coastal area which was called Brittany after them. Now the Anglo-Saxons built fortresses ('burh') throughout the country. Originally the word 'burh' meant a settlement fortified by palisades, earthworks and a ditch; a good example is Wallingford Castle in Berkshire. It is interesting to recall in this context that at that time London, the Roman Londinium, was called Lunderburh. In the 19th century England suffered the raids of the Danish invaders, the Vikings. During the following two centuries it became a semi-Danish country. The Danes brought with them to England a new form of large-scale enclosing wall, the remains of which can still be seen today in Willington, Bedfordshire. The Romans, Anglo-Saxons and Danes built their fortresses to protect the state, trade, and the local settlements, as had been the purpose of the prehistoric earthworks. They were in no way intended to protect individual feudal lords.

In 1066 Duke William of Normandy landed in England and defeated the Anglo-Saxon king Harold at the Battle of Hastings. With the conquest of Anglo-Saxon England by the romanized Normans, England was drawn out of the sphere of Scandinavian influence and became a Western country subject to the Church of Rome. The first castles which served a purely feudal purpose appeared in England during Norman rule.

The many royal castles which now sprang up along the main routes of southern England represented a completely new type of fortification in England, the motte-and-bailey. The motte is an artificial mound of earth in the shape of a frustum, enclosed at the base and on top by a palisade and encircled by a ditch. In front of it is the bailey, at a lower level, protected by earthworks and a ditch. The earthworks were also surrounded by palisades. The motte and bailey were connected by a bridge. At the end of the 12th century the motte was surmounted by a wooden tower.

The Bayeaux Tapestry gives a good idea of the appearance of the motte-and-bailey castle at that time; the mottes of Pickering in Yorkshire or of Carisbrooke (Ill. 9) on the Isle of Wight are relatively well-preserved examples of these early castles. Clearly they were built according to the power and the requirements of their owners. They varied in size and it is fairly certain that the actual tower on the motte was built only for the lord, his family, and his close retinue while the bailey was probably used as a refuge for the local people and their cattle in times of unrest; it contained stables, barns, **35** storerooms and the kitchens.

35–37 *Eltz Castle, Rhineland-Palatinate.
Eltz Castle on the Eifel is one of the most
beautiful German castles, situated in a valley
beside the Mosel. It seems to grow organically
out of a long spur of the cliff, surrounded by
picturesque scenery. It has no main tower, nor
does it have an enclosing wall because of the
lack of space. Instead, the massive walls of the
castle houses take over this function. It is a
typical 'multi-family' castle: four separate
residential buildings enclose the small inner
courtyard and they were the joint property of
the 'Ganerben' or co-heirs. The aspect of the
inner courtyard (Ill. 37) is reminiscent of
some medieval towns and here too the existing
space is used fully by the construction of
projecting upper storeys. The castle incorporates elements dating from the 12th to the
16th centuries.*

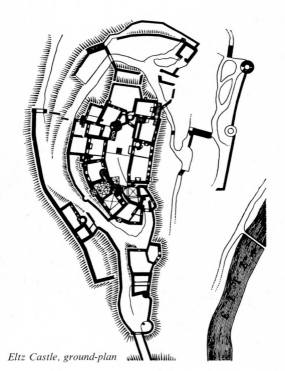

Eltz Castle, ground-plan

37

38 *Marksburg in Braubach on the Rhine. Marksburg, situated in an outstandingly beautiful landscape, overlooking the Rhine, was the only Rhenish castle that managed to withstand the sieges during the Thirty Years War. That is why it still stands as a complete example of the medieval German castle. It was begun in the early 13th century under the Count of Epstein and the first part to be built was the Bergfried tower. Round it are grouped the hall-range (Palas), the residential building known as the 'Rheinbau' and the 'Kaiser-Heinrich-Turm' (Emperor Henry Tower), which, however, dates from a much later period. The castle was used for the protection of the trade routes and customs privileges. From 1283 the castle overlords were the dynasty of Katzenelbogen who had obtained customs privileges from Rudolf of Habsburg. The name of the castle derives from the chapel of St Mark which was consecrated in 1437.*

Marksburg, ground-plan

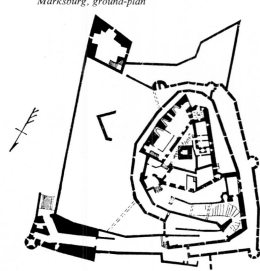

Barring a few exceptions (e.g. the stone keep of Fulk Nerra in Langeais dating from the late 10th century, Ill. 45), the castles of that period were built of wood, which was an advantage during invasions since they could be erected quickly, cheaply and without expert stonemasons. A report dating from the early 12th century describes a wooden castle of that type: 'Arnold, the Lord of Ardres, built a wooden house on the motte of Ardres which was made of more splendid building materials and was more beautifully timbered than any other house in Flanders at that time. The ground floor contained storerooms and granaries, great chests, vessels and other household utensils. On the floor above were the living quarters and the common rooms of the inmates, including the pantries, the rooms for the baker and the cellarer and the master bedroom of the lord and his wife. This adjoined the bedroom of the maids and the children. The large bedchamber also had a closed-off area in which a fire burned at dawn or in the evening or during illness or for bleeding or for the maids and small children to warm themselves . . . The

39–42 Chillon, Switzerland. The castle of Chillon stands on a low cliff by the eastern bank of Lake Geneva on a site fortified since early days. In the mid-13th century, Peter II of Savoy commissioned the architect Pierre Mainier to convert the earlier castle which is mentioned as early as 1150. Because of its favourable location, the castle only has flanking towers facing inland. Its main purpose was to control shipping on Lake Geneva. The interior, dating from the period when the castle was used as the residence of the counts of Savoy, was restored in the 20th century. The wooden ceilings (Ill. 41) are noteworthy, as is the cross-vaulting in the former prison (Ills. 40, 42) whose most famous prisoner was the Swiss humanist François de Bonivard (1493–1570).

40

upper storey contained the large attic rooms, where the lord's sons slept on one side, his daughters on the other. The guards and the servants who looked after the house also slept on this floor at various times of the day. High up on the east side of the house, at a well-situated spot, was the chapel, with a ceiling and paintings modelled on the Temple of Solomon. Steps and passages led from storey to storey, from the house to the kitchen, from room to room and also from the house into the loggia, where one could sit and enjoy conversation or leisure, and from the loggia to the chapel.' William the Conqueror had already had stone castles built in England, the best known of which is the White Tower of the Tower of London (Ill. 19) which was begun under the supervision of Gundolf of Bec, later bishop of Rochester, in 1070. This castle, symbol of the royal dignity and of the durability of the Norman conquests, was both a dungeon and a royal castle. Here the king held court and his chambers were hung with magnificent fabrics and decorated with wall paintings. Incidentally, the White Tower acquired its name because in the 13th century Henry III had it painted white – although it may already have been whitewashed at the time of William the Conqueror. This was the start of a style of building in England which was to culminate in some of the most impressive castles of the Middle Ages.

The English castle in the narrow sense of the word always has a keep. The keep is a high, towerlike structure containing the domestic and living quarters; usually it stands alone in the middle of the bailey enclosed by the outer wall and ditches. Its arrangement, form and function correspond to that of the French 'donjon' and to some extent also to the 'Bergfried' tower in German castles. At the beginning of the 12th century the palisade on the mound was replaced by a stone wall, which produced the so-called shell keep. Like the early French donjons, the keeps were rectangular. But soon it was realized – probably first in France – that this defensive method had drawbacks. For rectangular towers always had blind corners which offered the attackers shelter against arrows and other projectiles. A polygonal or

round tower avoided these sharp corners to some extent. The Christian crusaders probably became aware of the advantages of the round tower in the East.

Influences from the Near East are also evident in the castles which Edward I (1272–1307) built during the conquest of Wales. Skilful use of the lie of the land and the linking of wall and towers after Byzantine models characterize these 'Edwardian' castles and led to the construction of such mighty walled fortresses as Harlech (Ills. 26–29). Most of these castles were situated close to the sea to ensure supplies and the tactically important link between castle and fleet: it was a combined land and sea war that led to the defeat of the Welsh. The most important castles in Wales are Rhuddlan (1277–1282), Flint (1277–1285), Harlech (1283–1290, Ills. 26–29), Caernarvon (1285–1327, Ills. 30, 31), Beaumaris (1295–c. 1330) and Conway (1283–1389). Edward I's master builder was Jacques de Saint George who had previously spent sixteen years working for the Duke of Savoy; he now supervised all the building work in Wales and constructed the great, impregnable strongholds which were the expression of a strong central kingship in England.

The situation in Germany was quite different. With the weakening of the empire during the long dispute between pope and emperor the princes had gained in strength. The central power was split up into a number of regional administrative units. The general instability now also forced smaller landowners to protect themselves with fortifications. The influences from which the well-known type of the German medieval castle of the 11th century derived probably came via Lorraine. This type is the towered castle set on a hilltop whose predecessor, the motte-and-bailey castle, had emerged in England during the Norman conquest but had developed in a quite different manner there, as we have seen.

Perhaps the earliest surviving and dated tower castle in German-speaking Europe is Habsburg Castle, whose mighty, square tower-house was built in c. 1020 by the Alsatian Count Ratbold and his brother Bishop Werner of Strasbourg in Switzerland. In the tower castle, the residential tower is shifted to become the central structure and set on the motte. The southern German 'Wasserburg' also derived from the hilltop tower, except that here the motte encloses a whole system of waterways.

The primitive towers of the German early medieval castles could only be reached via a raised entrance. Unlike the French donjon and the English keep they were not always inhabited and were probably used mainly for the safe-keeping of moveable property and as a refuge in times of danger. They could be defended from a platform with battlements and appear to have been impregnable except with wall-breaking engines. But it was only when the enclosing wall was connected to the castle, thus uniting the defensive and residential areas in a single structure, that we find the well-known type of German castle. More castles were built in the German-speaking areas than anywhere else in Europe, especially by the Hohenstaufen (1138–1254; so-called after Hohenstaufen Castle in Swabia). The decrease and decentralization of royal power and the simultaneous growth in power of the princes and of the lower nobility prevented the emergence of a uniform, externally recognizable type of castle as found in England and France. The German castles were used to protect the property of noble families; they were usually given in tenure to the lord's liegemen and were smaller and more modest than the seats of the high nobility. The Hohenstaufen built a great number of castles of this kind in Alsace and in the Palatinate during the 12th century (e.g. Hohkönigsburg, Ortenburg, Trifels).

Soon a number of castles were built throughout Germany on the model of the

Hohenstaufen castles, and in spite of later alterations much of the original nucleus remains essentially the same today. It has been calculated that between the 11th and 15th century some 10,000 castles were built in German-speaking Europe, an astonishing achievement in view of the fact that most of them were erected high up on the hills.

One very beautiful example is the only undamaged castle on the Rhine, Marksburg at Braubach (Ill. 38). The nucleus of this castle, situated in a very lovely landscape, is the mighty rectangular Bergfried tower which clearly reveals its links with the earlier tower castle; the substructure dates back to the misty past while the cylindrical tower itself dates from the 13th century. The 'Palas' or hall-range was not built until *c.* 1400. These two structures and a second tower on the south corner are the dominant elements of the castle which was refortified and further extended for centuries. For instance, eastern and southern fortifications were added in the 17th century. From 1283 on the castle belonged to the counts of Katzenelnbogen. The name Marksburg is taken from the Chapel of St Mark consecrated in 1437.

One of the most beautiful German castles is Eltz (Ills. 35–37) in the Eifel, a valley beside the Mosel. Unlike Marksburg it does not have an isolated, dominant tower but consists of several residential towers which form a charming backdrop to the wooded landscape and the oldest of which, the so-called Platteltz, is mentioned in documents as early as 1263. Since the site on the long, steep ridge of rock was not large enough, the castle has no enclosing wall and the houses are clustered together on the slope in such a way that their outer walls assume the function and at times the appearance of a castle wall.

An outstanding example of the waterside castle is Chillon (Ills. 39–42) built on a low cliff by the eastern bank of Lake Geneva. This castle, first mentioned in 1150, was converted by the Duke of Savoy in the mid-13th century. The moat between the side of the lake and the castle is 20 m wide. The offensive wall opposite the shore is very strongly fortified with three semi-circular projecting angle towers with numerous embrasures and machicolations. Both walls of the keep have wall-walks. The masonry is made of superficially squared or unsquared quarry stone. The interior, which was thoroughly restored this century, is noted for the splendid wooden ceilings of the Palas (Ill. 41).

When considering the architectural features of the medieval German castle, a distinction is drawn between defensive and residential structures. The defensive structures include the enclosing wall, towers and gate, the residential structures are the Palas, the living quarters and the domestic buildings.

The enclosing wall, usually surmounted by a covered wall-walk, encircles the entire site. It is the earliest and simplest form of stone fortification. Characteristic of many Hohenstaufen castles of the 12th century is the use of rough-hewn rusticated masonry. Firstly, this made it more difficult for the enemy to raise the scaling-ladders and secondly it saved the time taken to work the stones completely smooth. The rusticated stone gives these castles a very monumental aspect. Small embrasures were let into the enclosing wall for observation and shooting at the enemy. After the crusades it became customary to surround the castle with a second, weaker wall. The small strip of land between the two walls forms an outer court. This made it difficult to bring the ramming engines up to the main enclosing wall, especially since there was generally also a moat outside the outer wall. If the besiegers managed to break through the first wall they could be attacked effectively from both flanks and from above on the enclosing wall inside this courtyard instead of the battle taking place within the precincts of the actual castle. The angles of the walls were often crowned with towers either for enfilades to

protect the enclosing wall or to protect the gates.

The most important defensive structure of the castle was the 'Bergfried' (Berchfrit), a term coined in the 19th century for the main tower of the German castle. It served both as watchtower and as final refuge. Sometimes several such towers were erected in one castle. The usual groundplan was a circle or a square although other shapes appear occasionally. The lowest floor usually housed the dungeons, the upper ones being used as guard rooms or for stairways. The entrance was high up, usually above the ground floor and was reached by a ladder or narrow steps. Other tower-like elements of these castles are bays (for drainage, latrines or for living accommodation) which were built onto towers and walls for technical purposes or simply as architectural ornaments; sometimes they were supported by consoles.

The position of the gates which served as entrance through the enclosing wall into the interior of the castle was determined by the terrain and the type of building. The gate was protected by wings reinforced with iron bands, by a portcullis and by a drawbridge, though the latter obviously only features if the castle is surrounded by a moat. Sometimes the gatehouse forms a separate structure and at times it is flanked by two towers for lateral defence. Often it is decorated with architectural ornaments and especially the lord's coat of arms.

The 'Palas' or hall is the main building of a castle. The name comes via the French 'palais', the Latin 'Palatium', the Palatine hill of Rome with its imperial 'palaces'. The rectangular Palas was usually built over a cellar and on two storeys, with the great knights' hall on the upper level. This is where assemblies and festivities were held. As the most important building it was richly decorated.

The private life of the lord and his family was confined to the residential quarters, for the Palas was only rarely inhabited. Usually they lived in a gabled house of several storeys and it too was richly ornamented.

The outhouses, stables, barns and storerooms were usually situated in the enclosure behind the drawbridge. The servants' quarters were sometimes also located there unless the servants lived in the main castle, where their quarters were of course far simpler than those of the lord.

The chapel occupied a special position among the important structures of the medieval castle. It could be free-standing or be situated within the Palas or an adjacent building. At any rate each castle had a chapel, richly decorated with wall-paintings.

The nature of the terrain, the organic growth of the castle buildings and the ever changing architectural style make the entire complex very picturesque from the outside but also from within the courtyard, although this must not deceive one about the actual conditions and circumstances of daily life in the Middle Ages. So it came that the painters and poets of the Romantic period rediscovered 'venerable witnesses to a proud past' in the castles that had fallen into ruin and oblivion since the late Middle Ages. In the wake of this romantically coloured rediscovery of the Middle Ages came the period of scientific research into castles as a result of which many castles which until then were often used merely as quarries were restored; in the 19th century we even find new castles modelled on those of the Middle Ages being built, such as Hohenschwangau near Füssen in Bavaria (Ill. 43). There is evidence that the lords of Schwangua had a castle on that site as early as the 12th century. This castle was altered a number of times and destroyed during the Napoleonic wars. Between 1833 and 1837 crown prince Maximilian, the future King Maximilian II of Bavaria, had a new castle built after the plans of the scene-painter Domenico Quaglio. With its four-towered Palas, this castle harmonizes well with the lovely landscape. The paintings in the rooms, some designed by Moritz von Schwind, depict historical and legendary subjects.

90

44 Neuschwanstein. Ludwig II, King of Bavaria and son of Maximilian II who built Hohenschwangau, commissioned the architect Eduard Riedel to build a medieval castle from the designs of the king and the scene-painter Christian Jank. The building, begun in 1868, fuses elements from the Romanesque and the Early Gothic styles and is reminiscent of Wartburg which Ludwig had visited in 1867. This late and expensive echo of the medieval castles represents a flight into a transfigured past at a time long after the industrial revolution had produced an entirely different society and culture.

The son of Maximilian II, King Louis II, began the building of a castle (Ill. 44) east of Hohenschwangau in 1868 in the Romanesque and early Gothic style and incorporating elements of Wartburg, which he had visited in 1867. He too used the designs of a scene-painter, Christian Jank. Originally the castle was called Neu-Hohenschwangau and the name Neuschwanstein was not used until 1890, four years after the king had drowned in the Starnberger Lake. This late and expensive echo of the medieval castle represented a flight into a completely transfigured past at a time long after the invention of the steam engine (1769), the railway (1814), the telegraph (1809), the telephone (1861), electric light (1879) and the motor car (1883). However, the magnificent and luxurious interiors of these castles have nothing in common with the medieval originals.

As a rule medieval castles were uncomfortable and unpleasant to live in. Since there were no windows in the outer walls but only embrasures for reasons of protection, the rooms were dark, dank and cold. The windows looking over the courtyard were barricaded with thin plates of horn in the winter which let in very little light. The only light in the long winter evenings was provided by oil lamps and pitch torches. The smoking hearths could not warm the draughty rooms which were furnished very sparsely with a couch, benches and chests; tables were only carried in at mealtimes. Carpets existed since the crusades but they could not have added very much to the comfort of the dark rooms. So daily life was generally conducted out of doors, weather permitting. Tournaments alternated with hunts in the forests unless the knights were obliged to take part in military expeditions. But even this life was not very comfortable and certainly not luxurious. The imperial knight and humanist Ulrich von Hutten (1488–1523) described the life in a castle very vividly: 'You must not take your life (that of a patrician in Nuremberg) as the yardstick for mine; even if I had a rich inheritance from my father so that I could live entirely off my own means, the unrest associated with our class would not allow me any leisure. We spend our time in the fields, in the woods, in the castles on top of hills. The people from whom we derive our maintenance are very poor peasants to whom we lease our fields, vineyards, meadows and woods. The yield from all this is very small in relation to the labour expended, but one works and toils to make it as large as possible, for we must be very careful householders. We also serve a prince from whom we hope for protection; if I did not do so, people would think they could treat me any old how. But even for the servant of a prince this hope is bound up with danger and fear every day. For as soon as I set foot out of the house, there is a danger of meeting people with whom the prince has quarrels and feuds and of them attacking and capturing me. If I am unlucky, I will have to hand over half my fortune in ransom, and so the protection I hoped for turns into loss. That is why we keep horses and buy weapons and surround ourselves with numerous followers, all of which costs a great deal of money. At the same time we cannot leave any fields undefended for long, we cannot visit a farm unarmed, and when we go hunting and fishing we have to wear a suit of armour.

The disputes between our peasants and others are unending; not a day goes by without reports of quarrels and strife which we then try to settle with the greatest caution. For if I defend my people too obstinately or actually pursue injustice, feuds will start; but if I let something pass too patiently, or even renounce what is due to me, then I expose myself to unjust attacks from all sides since what I have tolerated once is immediately claimed by all as reward for their presumption. And between what sort of people does all this happen? Not between strangers, my friend, but between relatives, cousins and even brothers. Those are the pleasures of our country life, our leisure, our rest. Whether a castle stands on a hill or on the plain, it is in any case not built for comfort but for defence, enclosed by ditches and a wall; we are suffocatingly cramped inside, penned in together with cattle and horses, and the dark rooms are stuffed full of heavy guns, pitch, sulphur and other weapons and war material. The gunpowder stinks everywhere and the scent of the dogs and their dirt is scarcely very charming either, in my opinion. And what a row! The sheep bleat, the cattle low, the dogs bark, the workers shout in the fields, the wagons and carts creak; and here at home, living as we do near the woods, we can hear the wolves howl.

Every day one thinks and worries about the morrow, we are in constant movement, never at rest. The fields have to be dug and then dug again, there is work to be done in the vineyards, trees have to be planted, meadows irrigated, the soil has to be turned, sown, fertilized, the corn has to be cut and threshed; now is the time of the harvest, then comes the vintage. If it is a bad year, as happens all too often in this infertile area, there is dreadful misery and poverty. Then there is nothing but worry, confusion, fear, friction and irritation hour after hour.'

France: From the Castle to the Château

The castles of medieval Europe have much in common because of the common needs of feudal society. This is especially true in England, France and Germany, typical feudal states. But at the same time the fortified places in these three countries also have certain individual features determined by their different national history. It makes a certain difference, for example, whether or not the area in question was originally under Roman rule. In addition, geographic and climatic differences produced national divergences in the building of castles. The centralized feudalism of Norman England, for instance, where the king alone had the right to build, and the feudal individualism of early medieval France led to different developments in castle architecture; German castles, for instance, look much more like fortresses while the later French ones are more palatial, which is why they are often referred to as châteaux rather than castles.

The first castles were built in France in the 9th and 10th centuries during the repeated invasions of the Normans, Hungarians, Saracens and many others.

45   Langeais, Indre-et-Loire. In the park of the château of Langeais stands the oldest keep in France, built by Fulk Nerra at the end of the 10th century. It is a good example of defensive building in the transitional period between wooden and stone keeps.

93

46

They were designed to protect the landlord and his peasants against attacks.
These castles were built either on a hill or on a raised mound. The towers and
the walls which were erected on the mound and enclosed the towers like
barricades were made of wood. Even at the beginning of the 12th century
when the Capetian King Louis VI the 'Fat' (1108–1137) broke the resistance
of the nobles in the Ile-de-France, castles could quite easily be taken simply by
firing. From about 1100 we find stone walls taking over, thus giving more
solidity and protection against fire. The earliest surviving example in France
is the ruined 'donjon' (keep) in the gardens of the castle of Langeais (Ill. 45)
some 25 km west of Tours.

The present castle of Langeais (Ill. 46, 47) was built by Jean Bourre in the 15th
century by order of Louis XI. The outer façade is characterized by the severity
of the sturdy round towers, with few apertures, while the inner façade facing
the stylized French gardens is relieved by the charming, typically late
medieval array of turrets and window gables. In contrast, the grey ruin of the
old keep situated on the mound at the end of the gardens surrounded by trees
expresses an inflexible harshness in brusque counterpoint to the inner façade
of the new château. Only the outer walls survive of the keep, built by Fulk
(Foulques) Nerra in 994/95. Fulk Nerra (the black), who became count of
Anjou at the age of 17, continued to feud and wage war until his old age. As an
old man he galloped from Angers to Saumur, intervened in a fight and,
without stopping, rode back to Angers. He was a curious mixture of brutality,
unscrupulousness and Christian humility and remorse. He extended the
county of Anjou with its capital of Angers to four times its size, consolidated
his rule by building a great many castles and keeps, had churches built, made
donations to the monasteries and went on three pilgrimages to Jerusalem.
According to the Anjou family chronicle, he had 13 castles built, and from
other documents it may be assumed that he also built 24 others, together with
a number of churches and monasteries which could take over the functions of
a fortress in times of war. Historians have called him the 'greatest builder of

4

48

48 *Langeais, Indre-et-Loire. From the outside, the château of Langeais gives the effect of a massive castle from feudal times. Seen from the inner courtyard – view of a door here – it looks more like a 15th-century princely residence.*

49 *Langeais, Indre-et-Loire. Unlike most of the châteaux on the Loire, Langeais is still furnished entirely in the style of its time. The furnishings give a good idea of château life in the 15th century. Although the castle had been built as protection against the Breton raids, this proved unnecessary a mere 22 years after its completion with the wedding in Langeais between Charles VIII and Anne of Brittany which took place here in 1491.*

49

50

50 *Montrichard, Loire-et-Cher. The keep was built in the 11th century by Fulk Nerra, the count of Anjou; it was renovated in the 12th century and later demolished by Henry IV.*

fortifications' and in fact few military leaders can have concerned themselves so deeply with building up a defensive system of castles. Besides the keep of Langeais, further evidence of his activity can be seen in the castles of Montbazon, Montrichard (Ill. 50), Montrésor and Loches (Ills. 52, 53). All except Langeais were rebuilt later and expanded, but even today they all have in common the massive, rectangular keep as the main structure, often without the enclosing walls normally used for defensive purposes. The rectangular keep is generally on three levels. The ground floor was used as a windowless storeroom, kitchen or prison. On the first floor, which was usually also the entrance floor, were the lord's hall and living quarters and on the second floor the quarters of the women and children.

Naturally, keeps of this kind are not all based on the ground plans of Fulk Nerra. At the beginning of the development of fortification building, the wooden keeps gradually gave way to stone keeps for greater protection against fire and enemies.

A good example is the keep of Beaugency (Ill. 51) in the domain of the count of Blois, the powerful eastern enemy of the count of Anjou. Beaugency keep is similar to that of Loches (Ill. 53). It dates from the 11th century when keeps were still built on a rectangular ground plan and supported by buttresses; round keeps are not found until later. Beaugency keep had five floors, although the interior is now destroyed.

The keep of Loches (Ills. 52, 53) was also built in the 11th century. It was intended to protect the threatened south flank of the Cité, the fortifications outside the town. It stands 37 m high and its walls are reinforced by buttresses. On his return from the Third Crusade, the English King Richard the Lionheart had fallen into the hands of the German Emperor Henry VI after being shipwrecked at Aquilia and recognized at Dürnstein on the Danube in spite of his disguise. Richard was held captive in Trifels Castle in the Palatinate until 1194 when the emperor freed him for a high ransom. At that time the French king Philip II Augustus had managed to obtain Loches from Richard's brother John. So after his release Richard the Lionheart hurried to Loches where he reconquered the castle in the space of three hours. In 1205 Philip Augustus counter-attacked but he had to besiege the castle for a year before re-occupying it.

There were probably a number of similar fortified buildings in the Duchy of Normandy, for this alone would account for the fact that the castles which William the Conqueror and his successors built in England follow the same basic ground plan of a rectangular keep (cf. the White Tower, the keep of the Tower of London [Ill. 19], and the Norman keep of Kenilworth [Ill. 25]). The rectangular ground plan of the early feudal keeps was soon abandoned since it had blind corners which offered relative protection to attackers. This drawback was particularly serious in the early days when irregular, very roughly hewn stone and mortar of poor quality were used. Fortifications of this type also had other disadvantages, like the absence of a courtyard surrounded by solid enclosing walls which could serve as a refuge for the local peasants, and the absence of stables for the horses which were so essential to the knights.

The first attempts to solve this problem led to the round tower, a system which the knights had discovered during the crusades in the East in the 11th century. A typical example of the new building methods learned by the crusaders is Krak des Chevaliers in Syria (Ill. 2), the castle of the Hospitallers. Round towers were now used as architectural principle not only of keeps; they were also added to the four corners of a main tower and later the enclosing wall was also equipped with protruding round towers. A good example of this kind of extended tower complex is the 45 m-high Tour de César (Ill. 55) built on a mound near Provins in Champagne in the 12th century.

98

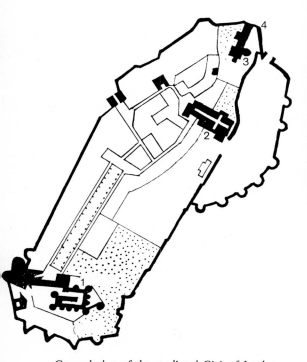

Ground-plan of the medieval Cité of Loches
1 *Keep*
2 *St-Ours*
3 *'Tower of Agnes Sorel'*
4 *Royal apartments*

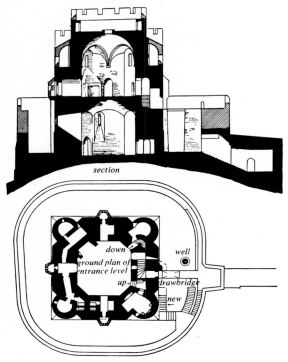

Provins (cf Ill. 55), section and ground-plan of the keep ('Tour de César')

53

The astonishing progress in building techniques in the 12th century can be followed most clearly in Romanesque church architecture, but the history of fortress building also pursued a remarkable development in the second half of the 12th century. Examples include the Chinon castles of Henry II Plantaganet (1154–1189, great-grandson of Fulk Nerra), King of England and heir to Anjou, Maine, Touraine and Normandy; and Gaillard castle which the son of Henry II, Richard I the Lionheart, built on the lower course of the Seine to defend Normandy against the raids of the French Capetians. These castles were built by the English but it is quite justifiable to regard them as links in the chain of French fortifications since initially (second half of the 12th century until the coronation of Edward I in 1272) the English rulers of the Plantagenet dynasty were more French than English. They were in fact the real rulers of western France (Kingdom of the Angevines).

Chinon is famous as the place where Joan of Arc first met the dauphin Charles, the future Charles VII (1422–61), on 9 March 1429. Charles, the 'King of Bourges', had established his small court in Chinon since Henry VI, King of England, was also the 'King of Paris'. This enormous castle complex, situated on a hill and extending 400 m from east to west and 70 m north to south, was built according to the plans of Henry II who died there and was buried in Fontevrault. It consists in fact of three castles separated by moats: Fort St Georges, the Château du Milieu, and the Château du Coudray with the keep where Joan of Arc once lived on the first floor. The French King Philip II Augustus (1180–1223) besieged this castle for eight months in 1205 before capturing it.

Château Gaillard (Ill. 56) built on a steep cliff over the Seine, still looks impregnable today. It was built in 1196 by Richard the Lionheart. The round main towers were flanked by a number of small round towers, as was the splendid curtain wall. The French army of Philip II Augustus managed to take this castle in 1203 in spite of the fierce resistance of its defenders and of King John of England. It only succeeded because the French soldiers discovered the latrine shaft which led down through the wall into the Seine and managed to invade the castle by climbing up in the dark of the night. The 13th century was the time of the great French Gothic cathedrals. Now the

101

54 Loches, Indre-et-Loire. The royal residence ('Logis Royaux'), built in two stages in the 14th and 15th centuries, is situated in the northern part of the City. Shown on the left is the older and higher part ('Vieux Logis') with its four projecting round towers linked to each other by a wall-walk, still looking entirely like a feudal castle. To the left is the 'Tower of the Beautiful Agnes' after Sorel, mistress of Charles VII. On the right is the later part ('Nouveau Logis') of the castle, added by Charles VIII and Louis XII.

55 Provins, Seine-et-Marne. The 'Tour de César, a huge 12th-century keep, is 45 m high. It is a good example of the more complex manner of constructing these keeps making use of what had been learned in the East during the crusades. The projecting round towers made it possible to attack any assailants who had penetrated as far as the curtain walls.

pointed arch came into use everywhere, relieving and articulating the heavy Romanesque walls. The cathedral walls had little supportive function now, the weight being carried instead by numerous buttresses; this meant that the walls could be made thinner and opened up by windows and other apertures. Although this style was not applied directly to castle building since it was largely the solidity of walls that guaranteed good defence, the advanced building technique offered certain advantages for building fortifications too. Philip Augustus, who defeated the king of England at the Battle of Bouvines in 1214 and took over his possessions north of the Loire, was the first king of that period to manage to combine all the royal power in his own hand. He completed the fortifications of the royal palace on the Ile de la Cité in Paris which now houses the Ministry of Justice. The palace itself was only completed under King Louis IX, St Louis (1226–1270).

Many of the castles of this period still survive in part at least. Most have a rectangular ground plan with enormous towers on the four corners (rectangular castles). No efforts were spared now to avoid blind corners on the walls. Beside the tranditional keeps, we now also find more complex structures in which the condition of the land was taken ever more into account when the enclosing walls were built. Sometimes there were even two enclosing walls. They were surrounded outside by deep moats which could only be crossed by drawbridge. The gate, flanked by two towers, was protected by a double wooden or iron door and a portcullis. There were also embrasures above and beside the gateways for better defence against approaching attackers. Sometimes the ground floor of the round keep could be reached directly but usually the only access was from the second floor by a ladder which could be drawn up in case of danger. Unlike the Bergfried in German castles, the donjon was designed from the start as a fortified residential tower and as the permanent residence of the lords – not just as a watch tower – and as a final refuge in times of need. Eventually the castle complex came to include more residential buildings, the 'corps de logis' and the 'avant corps' attached to the domestic quarters ('communs'). This extended type of castle could resist sieges for longer and more effectively. The enclosing wall was surmounted by battlements to allow the defenders to shoot from protected places and wall-walks were constructed so that the garrison could move round the castle quickly and easily; sometimes the wall-walk projected over consoles for better attack of any assailants who had come close up to the wall.

A good example of the rectangular castle in France in the Gothic High Middle Ages was the Bastille in Paris which was destroyed during the French Revolution in 1789. There is also a castle in Italy which can serve as a fairly exact illustration of the building style of the Bastille, the Castel Nuovo in Naples (Ill. 71) which a French master builder erected for Charles of Anjou (1226–1285), the king of Naples, in 1279–1282. Another very impressive example of the medieval fortress is the château of Angers (Ill. 57), the old capital of Anjou. Shortly after this county was annexed to France, Blanche de Castille and her son St Louis had the old castle of the Plantagenets rebuilt in 1228–1238 as protection against the English, and Angers became one of the mightiest outposts of the French kingdom. Unfortunately, all that remains today is the huge enclosing wall and the chapel, built at the beginning of the 15th century by Louis II of Anjou and his wife Yolande of Aragon, with its magnificent Late Gothic vaulting. The enclosing wall with its 17 enormous circular towers follows an irregular pentagon; it was built of slabs of slate alternating with courses of sandstone and granite. Although the towers, originally with conical roofs, were lowered by two storeys, even now they stand between 40 m and 50 m high. Towards the end of the 16th century the fortress was to have been demolished under Henry III, but the governor

Pages 104–105:
56 Chateau Gaillard, Eure, rises on a steep cliff above the Seine. The castle was built in 1196 by King Richard the Lionheart and occupied in 1203 by the French King Philip II Augustus. The keep which still towers over the ruins was once surrounded by a very extensive defensive system.

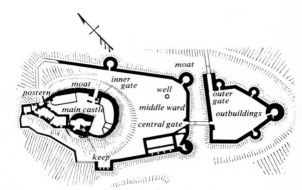

Chateau Gaillard, ground-plan

57 Angers, Maine-et-Loire. Angers castle is a particularly impressive example of medieval fortified building. In 1228–1238 Blanche of Castile and her son, St Louis, refortified the old Roman city walls dating from the 3rd century and also rebuilt the old castle of the counts of Anjou. The enclosing wall of the fortress is defended by 17 large towers which still stand between 130 and 160 ft high although two storeys were taken down under Henry III. The wall, built of slate, sandstone and granite and reminiscent of the inland-facing walls of Constantinople, is surrounded by a moat originally filled with water.

delayed the destruction for so long that the death of the king in 1589 saved parts of it. Under Louis XIV it was used as state prison, later as a powder magazine and arsenal. The château of Angers is a particularly good example of the sober and monumental beauty of French fortifications in the 12th and 13th centuries. This building, designed entirely for defensive purposes, has a functional beauty which clearly reflects the general outlook on life and the world of the feudal lords of the time.

The medieval French feudal château is still based on the model of a castle with battlements, wall-walks, embrasures and machicolations, but combines these defensive elements with an astonishing feeling for comfort. The ground plan is generally a closed rectangle and basically the construction differs little from that of earlier castles. But the ornamentation shows that the château now increasingly took account of aesthetic requirements. Even from the outside this is evident in the number of pointed turrets, while in the interior the living quarters have become more spacious and comfortable; there are also more and larger windows which relieve the external façade and lighten the interior. The château of Pierrefonds in Compiègne, dating from the late 14th century, which Viollet le Duc restored in the 19th century from surviving documents, and the château of Saumur are splendid examples of this late medieval defensive architecture.

Saumur lies on the Loire, some 60 km south of Tours. The town is known for its wines and its schools of cavalry. After the Norman attacks the inhabitants sought refuge on the mountain ridge between the Loire and Thouet. The nucleus of the present château (Ill. 58) goes back to 10th-century fortifications although the interior was rebuilt at the end of the 14th century by René of Anjou and fortified even more strongly in the 16th century. Louis XIV turned it into a state prison. Later it was used as a powder magazine, barracks and arsenal until it fell into ruin in the 19th century. In 1906 the town had the château thoroughly restored and housed two museums in it. Originally it was in the form of a closed rectangle round the courtyard. Later one wing was pulled down and replaced by a terrace giving a charming view over the Loire valley. There are defensive towers on the corners of the wall, round below and octagonal above, with a wall-walk and machicolations. The original aspect of the building can still be seen in one of the illuminations of the Book of Hours of the Duc de Berry. In terms of military architecture, this fortress stands on the threshold between the Middle Ages and modern times.

The defiant keep of the château of Vincennes (Ill. 59) is quite unlike more decorative castles such as Saumur. On the western side of the Forest of Vincennes where the Capetian kings used to go hunting and where St Louis sat in judgement under an oak tree, the kings of the Valois dynasty built a castle in 1337–1373 on the foundation walls of a 12th century fortification in order to protect Paris. The general layout is a large, regular rectangle with a wide interior courtyard. The great keep is on the west side with masonry over 3 m thick and flanked at the corners by large round towers. It was arranged on six storeys and contained the living quarters of the royal family. Wide steps led up to the second floor, the other floors being reached by spiral stairs. Later a separate house was erected for the royal family.

During the Hundred Years War (1339–1453) many castles changed in appearance. With the invention of firearms, defensive techniques had to be rethought which finally led to a fundamentally different kind of fortification. Hardly a single 13th-century castle remained in its original form and the châteaux which were built after the Hundred Years War were not so much castles as showpieces. The medieval feudal castle ('château fort') gave way to the country château or pleasure seat ('château de plaisance') which still has some fortified aspects but no real military significance. The châteaux on the Loire very clearly illustrate the change from the military castle to the residential and display building.

108

58 Saumur, Maine-et-Loire. The château of Saumur was begun in the late 14th century by Louis I of Anjou and completed under Louis II of Anjou. It is interesting to compare this building with the castle depicted in the Book of Hours of the Duc de Berry (illustration of the month of September) dating from c. 1410.

Page 110:
59 Vincennes, Seine. The six-storey keep was the main structure of a castle which the Valois family built in 1337–1373 as protection for Paris in the forest of Vincennes. The royal apartments were in the keep, which is 170 ft high with walls over 9 ft thick and a moat around it 46 ft deep. It is further protected by projecting round angle-towers.

The courtyard of the château of Blois (Ill. 60–63) retraces the history of French castle and château architecture from the time of St Louis to that of Louis XIII. The earliest parts date from the 13th century: a round tower on the castle wall and the Hall of the Estates ('salle des états'), in which the Estates General met twice during the Huguenot wars. Opposite lies the sober gallery of Charles of Orleans dating from the mid-15th century, alongside the chapel of Saint-Calais, the royal private chapel which Louis XII had rebuilt

60–63 Blois, Loire-et-Cher. The courtyard of the château of Blois illustrates the history of French castle and château architecture from the time of St Louis to that of Louis XIII. The Louis XII wing (Ill. 60) dates from c. 1500. The most impressive wing is that of Francis I, dating from 1515–1524 (Ill. 63: outer façade of the loggia) with its stairway projecting in front of the façade facing the courtyard (Ill. 62). The architectural ornamentation here consists of Francis I's heraldic animal, the salamander (Ill. 61).

Pages 116–117:
64 Chaumont-sur-Loire. After the repeated destruction of earlier fortresses on this site, this château was built in 1465–1510, in the transitional style between Gothic and Renaissance. Catherine de' Medici, widow of King Henry II, acquired the château in 1560 and exiled Diana of Poitiers, the mistress of the late king, there.

between 1498 and 1503. The Louis XII wing dates from the same time (Ill. 60). The most expensive and impressive wing is that of Francis I, with a magnificent stairway in front (Ill. 62) dating from 1515–1524. The latest part of the building is the wing of Gaston of Orleans dating from 1635–38 (from designs by François Mansart). After Louis XII the Italian influence is very evident in French château architecture. In spite of the many different building phases, the château of Blois has a uniform and harmonious aspect; it is more Gothic then Renaissance – apart from the Gaston of Orleans wing which is entirely in the Classical style. This is a case where the defensive and military building of a medieval feudal lord was transformed over the centuries into a royal château which was to have a decisive influence on subsequent French château architecture.

Important events of French history are bound up with Blois. It was the preferred residence of Duke Charles of Orleans (1391–1465) who was captured by the English at the Battle of Agincourt and not released for 25 years. He himself was a poet of repute and he surrounded himself at Blois with a circle of artists and scholars, including François Villon at one time. His son, King Louis XII, made Blois into a royal residence which played a role similar to that of Versailles later. The rule of Henry III (1574–1589) was the most dramatic period in the history of the town. During the Huguenot wars the Estates General met here twice (1576 and 1588) and this is where Henry III had the powerful Duke of Guise, leader of the radical Catholic League, murdered in 1588. After the murder of Henry III eight months later, the Bourbons mounted the French throne with Henry of Navarre. in 1617 Mary de' Medici was exiled to Blois by her son Louis XIII. But in spite of her large girth she managed to escape one night by descending into the castle moat by rope ladder. In 1626 Louis XIII presented the County of Blois to his brother, Duke Gaston of Orleans, in order to remove this rival to the throne from his court. Gaston of Orleans, leader of the resistance against Richelieu and later against Mazarin, managed to indulge his ambitious building schemes for three years with state funds (architect: François Mansart); but then the king had a son which destroyed Gaston's hopes of the throne, whereupon the minister of state, Richelieu, also cut off his funds. This brought the building work on the château of Blois to a halt.

Also on the Loire, between Blois and Amboise, situated on a steep slope, lies the picturesque little village of Chaumont. The château of Chaumont (Ill. 64) combines medieval and Renaissance features. The whole complex with its round angle towers still adheres closely to the Middle Ages. Originally the building was in the shape of a rectangle truncated on the south-east corner. In the 18th century the wing facing the valley was pulled down, opening up a magnificent view over the Loire valley. The entrance from a corner is unusual. The earliest castle was built in the 10th century by Eudes I, Count of Blois, mainly as protection against Fulk Nerra, Duke of Anjou. In *c.* 1026 it passed into the possession of Gueudoin whose grand-daughter married Sulpice I of Amboise so that Chaumont passed to this family. In 1154 the castle was razed to the ground at the behest of the Count of Blois but it was rebuilt shortly after. In 1170 Henry II of England met Thomas Becket, Archbishop of Canterbury, here. On his return to England the archbishop had the king excommunicated whereupon the king hired assassins who stabbed him in his cathedral. Louis XI had Chaumont demolished during the disputes between the crown and the powerful feudal lords. (The present structure dates from 1465–1510.) Pierre d'Amboise, having regained the king's favour, was employed as master builder of the new building which was completed by Charles I of Amboise and Charles II. After the death of Henry II (1559) his widow, Catherine de' Medici, acquired Chaumont. She forced the king's mistress, Diana of Poitiers, to live here instead of at her château of

65, 66 *Amboise, Indre-et-Loire. The château is situated on a cliff ledge over the Loire which was fortified even in Roman times. Remnants of the Roman wall still survive. In the 11th century this was the site of two castles. Louis XI made Amboise the residence of the queen, Charlotte of Savoy, and it was here that King Charles VIII was later born. During his rule the entire plateau was reconstructed. The enclosed courtyard was covered in carpets during feasts and above it was spanned a sky-blue cloth decorated with sun, moon and stars. On this side of the enclosing wall stands the chapel of St Hubert which was originally part of the queen's apartments. For a long time it housed the remains of Leonardo da Vinci whom Francis I had brought to Amboise. Ill. 65 shows the north side of the château, viewed from the Loire, with the great balcony where the protestant conspirators were hanged (1560) after rebelling against the Duke of Guise.*

66

Chenonceaux. Incidentally the authoress Madame de Staël was also exiled to Chaumont by Napoleon at the beginning of the 19th century and lived there for some time with friends who included Madame Récamier, August Wilhelm Schlegel and the young Adalbert von Chamisso.

One of the most important châteaux on the Loire is Amboise (Ills. 65, 66). Like Blois it stands on the site of an earlier medieval castle. Charles VIII began to build the present château in 1492. On his return from his Italian campaign he brought a number of artists and scholars back to Amboise. From that time on the Italian Renaissance exerted a definite influence on French art and culture. Louis XII and Francis I continued the building after the tragic death of Charles VIII (on 7 April 1498 the king struck his head on a low gate during a ball game and a few hours later he suddenly fell unconscious and died). The only surviving wing of the original quadrangle dates from the time of Louis XII. Francis I received Charles V here. A sinister story is linked to this castle, bound up with the beginning of the Huguenot wars. It concerns the so-called Amboise conspiracy in which the allegedly Protestant plotters led by a nobleman called La Renaudie were hanged from the château balcony and battlements, drowned in the Loire, or decapitated and drawn and quartered. For a long time the body of Leonardo da Vinci, whom Francis I brought to Amboise, rested in the chapel of St Hubert.

The château of Chenonceaux (Ill. 67) was built in 1513–1521 by Thomas Bohier, the treasurer of Kings Charles VIII, Louis XII and Francis I. Formerly the land belonged to the de Marques family who were forced to sell it bit by bit. In the course of time Bohier managed to acquire the entire estate and had the old castle pulled down except for the keep. The new building above the river Cher rises on the foundations of a mill which had belonged to

67 *Chenonceaux, Indre-et-Loire. The new château was built by the royal treasurer Thomas Bohier in 1513–1521 on the foundations of an old water-mill. Twenty years earlier Bohier had gradually acquired the land of the former owner, the de Marques family. The only remains of the old castle is the keep (left). To the right, the treasurer's building with its four angle towers adjoins the two-storeyed gallery of Catherine de' Medici on the bridge over the Cher. Catherine took over the château of Diana of Poitiers, her husband the king's mistress, after Diana's death in 1559 and built magnificent extensions to it. Diana of Poitiers, who had been responsible for the construction of the bridge linking the main building with the opposite bank, was banned to Chaumont but only stayed there briefly before retiring to her château of Anet where she died seven years later.*

68 Chambord, Loire-et-Cher. This château in the forest of Boulogne is the largest of the châteaux of the Loire and in a sense the precursor of Versailles. Francis I had it built at great expense in 1519–1533. The four-towered keep and the enclosing wall recall the ground plan of the old type of feudal castles although this splendid Renaissance building in no way resembles a medieval castle. The lovely north-west façade, shown on this illustration, has all the characteristics of a royal pleasure seat.

69

69, 70 Avignon, Vaucluse. The papal palace in Avignon, dominating the city, stands on the threshold between castle and urban princely palace. It was built during the so-called 'Babylonian' captivity of the Church (1309–1377) when the popes resided in Avignon and were dependent on the French king. The popes' castle has all the defensive equipment of fortified buildings of that time: thick walls, towers crowned with pinnacles on projecting consoles, machicolations, etc. Left, in the foreground, the famous 'Pont St Benézét', called the 'Pont d'Avignon' (Ill. 69), destroyed in the 17th century, which originally spanned both arms of the Rhône on 22 arches (some 980 yards long). It was built in the 12th century and was one of the four bridges over the Rhône below Lyons across which the medieval pilgrims' and trade routes led from Italy to France, Spain, the Netherlands and England.

the old castle. It consists of a central structure with four corner towers and a great hipped roof. Bays and turrets relieve the solid mass of the building. The decoration is a harmonious combination of Late Gothic and Early Renaissance styles. On the death of Bohier in 1524 the château passed to Francis I since it turned out that the treasurer had been in debt to the state. When he came to the throne in 1547, Henry II gave the château to his mistress Diana of Poitiers, who had a splendid garden laid out and a bridge on four pillars built connecting it to the opposite bank of the Cher. After the king's death at a tournament in 1559 Diana had to cede Chenonceaux to his widow, Catherine de' Medici, and retired to the sombre castle of Chaumont where, however, she only stayed briefly before withdrawing permanently to her château of Anet. Catherine de' Medici eagerly continued to extend the château. She had a wide, two-storey gallery built after plans by Philibert Delormes on Diana's bridge, which was decorated in a modest, almost Classical style, in striking contrast to the splendour of the earlier building. Catherine held magnificent feasts which caused some sensation among her contemporaries and received Francis II, Mary Stuart and Charles IX there. She left the castle to her daughter-in-law, Louisa of Lorraine, wife of Henry III, who retired there for the rest of her life after the murder of the king in 1589. Later, Chenonceaux passed to the Dukes of Vendome, then to the Duke of Bourbon and in 1730 it came into the hands of a large estate owner called Dupin whose wife had a famous literary salon. Jean-Jacques Rousseau educated Madame Dupin's sons here and it was for her that he wrote the pedagogical novel 'Emile'; in his 'Confessions' he gratefully describes the happy time he spent at the château of Chenonceaux.

Perhaps the most beautiful and certainly the largest château on the Loire is Chambord (Ill. 68). It extends over an area of 156 m by 117 m, has 440 rooms, 365 chimneys, 800 capitals, 14 large and 60 small stairways, not counting the famous double-spiral stairway in the keep. The park is enclosed by a wall

Pages 126–127:
71 Naples. The fortress 'Castel Nuovo' was built by Charles I, Count of Anjou, in 1279–1282. Charles of Anjou, a younger brother of the French king Louis IX, who defeated the Hohenstaufen in southern Italy on behalf of the papacy, chose Naples as his capital after Sicily had risen in arms in the Sicilian Vespers Rising (1282) and massacred all the French in Sicily. Charles of Anjou brought the new French influences to bear on Italian castle building. So this mighty fortress is really an example of French defensive architecture, which is why it also resembles the Bastille destroyed in the French Revolution, the fortress at the gate of Saint-Antoine in Paris built 100 years later (1369–1382). Between the two great gatehouse towers rises the triumphal arch, built in 1455–1458 by L. Laurana in memory of the arrival of Alfonso I the Magnificent of Aragon who came to the throne of the kingdom of Sicily after the fall of the Anjou house in Italy in 1442, thus reuniting Naples and Sicily.

124

32 km long, the longest in France. But these figures give no idea of the overwhelming effect of the building which can be seen in the great forest of Boulogne rising at the end of a path like a fairytale castle. It has rightly been called a precursor of Versailles.

Francis I built the castle in 1519–1533, except for the work on the exterior which took longer. The ground plan is still based on the feudal model of a four-towered keep with a curtain wall, but the rectangular ground plan of the walls has been turned into four wings (three really, since the fourth side is formed by the keep and two galleries), with round towers at the corners. The high tent roofs and the various superstructures on them still hark back to the Middle Ages; but the severe articulation of the façades and the ornamentation reveal the orderly influence of the Renaissance. The great double spiral stairway which winds up through the crossing tower of the keep is a masterpiece of interior architecture and decoration. It consists of two adjacent, spirals enclosed in a skeleton shaft.

In 1539 Francis I held a magnificent reception in Chambord for Emperor Charles V and at the sight of the castle the emperor said: 'This castle is the essence of what the art of man can create.' In 1552 Margrave Moritz of Saxony, leader of the German opposition of princes, and Henry II of France entered into an alliance against the German emperor. On 15 January a treaty was signed at the château of Chambord whereby Toul, Metz and Verdun were ceded to France. In 1626 Louis XIII gave his brother Gaston of Orleans the County of Blois which also included Chambord. Under Louis XIV it reverted to the crown and the king stayed there on nine occasions. It was also at Chambord that Molière wrote 'Monsieur de Pourceaugnac' and 'Le Bourgeois Gentilhomme'. Both plays were staged there for the first time in the presence of Louis XIV, and until Versailles was completed Chambord remained his favourite royal palace. Louis XV placed it at the disposal of his father-in-law, Stanislaus Leszyzynski, the dethroned Polish king. Later he presented it to Marshal Moritz of Saxony in gratitude for his victory at Fontenoy, and the proud and hot-tempered marshal spent the rest of his life there.

In the development from castle to urban palace, the papal palace in Avignon and Marienburg on the Weichsel, the seat of the grand master of the order of Teutonic Knights 60 km south of Danzig, form transitional points. Marienburg was begun in 1280 when the order embarked on the conversion and subjection of the Prussians at the end of the crusades.

The papal palace in Avignon, Vaucluse (Ills. 69, 70), was built during the exile of the popes, the so-called 'Babylonian' captivity of the church (1309–1377). In 1305 the Archbishop of Bordeaux, Bertrand de Got, had been elected Pope Clement V. On the advice of the French King Philip IV the pope chose Avignon for his see because of the unrest in Rome. Later popes remained there too, partly under the pressure of the French king, partly because of the instability of the pontifical state. It was not until the beginning of 1377 that Gregory XI returned to Rome because resistance to the pope was becoming increasingly strong in Italy and the pontifical state was threatened with annihilation. The anti-popes Clement VII and Benedict XIII resided in Avignon until 1408 and during that time Avignon was transformed from a rather modest provincial town into a political centre where the arts flourished. It may seem surprising that the popes needed a fortified palace at all; but at that time they were also secular princes who ruled over land, which always involved the risk of armed conflict. That is why Pope Benedict XII (1334–1342) started the construction of a spacious palace which was extended and completed by his successor Clement I (1342–1352). The architect was Jean de Louvres from the south of France. The building, erected on a cliff near the cathedral in 1134–1352, is not based on a symmetrical ground plan and does not give an impression of unity, nor has it an obvious main façade. The only articulation of the huge masses of stone is achieved by a blind arcade which runs round the walls to their full height. Such monumental, solid walls were highly characteristic of the southern French building style; similarly, the defensive churches of Provence had walls relieved by niches in the 12th century (Les-Saintes-Maries, Palace of Narbonne). This gigantic papal stronghold, dominating the town, has all the defensive apparatus of the castles of the time: almost Cyclopean masonry, towers surmounted by battlements on projecting consoles, machicolations etc. The palace withstood several sieges although it was quite severely damaged. When Gregory XI moved the papal see back to Rome in 1377, the palace became the seat of the papal legates. Over the next centuries it fell into disrepair. During the French Revolution orders were given to tear it down, but this proved impossible because of its massive dimensions. For some years the palace was used as a prison and in 1818 was converted into barracks. In 1906 the town began to restore it. The château tradition in France had a decisive influence on the development of architecture in general after the Renaissance. The magnificent showpieces gave concrete expression to the strong French kingship, and were imitated in more modest fashion by the country nobility. The castle was no longer intended merely to protect the lord and his family but designed to house an impressive court with a retinue of hundreds: this required a far more grandiose system of building. So the development of the medieval castle comes to an end with the palace, which was to reach its full flowering in the Baroque period.

Towns and Burgesses

Development of the Medieval Town

Decisive economic, social, political and cultural changes took place in the medieval towns which were eventually to bring about the end of the Middle Ages and the beginning of modern times. Thanks to their economic power, the inhabitants of the towns, the burgesses, were able to withstand kings and noblemen and assert themselves as the 'third estate'.

The medieval town was characterized less by architectural and more by its economic and legal features. It was a place in which legally free inhabitants earned their living mainly from trade and the crafts, unlike the majority of unfree villagers who gained their livelihood from agriculture.

The real 'victors' of the crusades were the merchants and the trading towns. The newly emergent trade with the East produced a money economy which took over from the former 'natural' economy that had been an essential element of feudalism and from the barter system. The possession of money became a new form of wealth; until then wealth had meant ownership of land, which was largely vested in the ecclesiastical or royal power. The money economy now made it possible to accumulate capital which in turn made it possible to equip ships and instal stores for merchandise. The money economy first developed in areas where the trading towns were densest, in northern Italy and Flanders. As early as 1252 Florence minted the first Florentine gold florins ('fiorino d'oro'), the most sought-after coin in international trade. And it was in the northern Italian towns that the trade of money changer and banker, soon to spread throughout Europe, first appeared. One of the best-known and most famous banking families was that of the Medici in Florence who were later ennobled and were to control the destiny of the town for several centuries.

Capitalism, an economic structure based on the private ownership of the most important means of production, inevitably developed from the money economy, replacing feudalism, a system based on ownership of land by the nobility and the clergy and on the serfdom of the peasants. The main representatives of the capitalist economic structure, which at the time represented an enormous social advance, were the burgesses. They developed the new ideas which took over from the chivalric ideal, culminating later in those notions which still – so it is claimed, at least – characterize bourgeois society, namely democracy, freedom of the individual, the equality of all citizens and the fraternity of mankind. The feudal state, based on the allegiance of vassal to overlord, was followed by the bureaucratic state, whose officials were paid in money. The 12th century saw the first civil states in Europe: the Norman state in Sicily which Emperor Frederick II made into the most modern (absolutist) state in Europe in the 13th century, and France. Both adopted the model of the towns. The end of the feudal state also meant the end of the power of the nobility as representatives of feudalism. Monarchies emerged in the Norman states of England, Normandy and Sicily in which the nobility was more strictly subordinated to the monarch.

The emergence and strengthening of the bourgeoisie, a civil administration and a strong monarchy mark the new European national states, while the seat of power moved from the castle to the town.

During the period of the migration of nations, the German tribes had penetrated into Roman territory where they encountered an economic structure based on trade and the ownership of large estates. The Roman landowner would lease that part of his estate which he could not farm himself with the help of slaves to a tenant farmer. The community life of the Germans was also based on a relationship of dependence. That is why, during the migration of nations, the acquisition of land by the Germans meant only a change of owner, while ownership relations remained the same. The German nobles owned the land, while the farming was carried out by the landlord's serfs or by free peasants who had to pay him in compulsory labour service and dues. The part of the landowner's estate providing for his own needs was farmed by his peasants, serfs who could be sold or inherited like private property. The number of free peasants with their own land continually dwindled. The nobleman who had enough land for his needs and could increase his reserves by appropriating new land (unowned land, cleared woodland) made it available to free men in return for certain dues and also granted them legal and military protection. Most peasants were serfs, that is they were bound to the landlord and his land by compulsory service and dues and were not permitted to leave. In the 12th century Godfrey of Troyes described the life of the peasants as follows: 'The peasants who work for everyone, who drudge all the time and carry out services disdained by their lord all the year round are constantly harassed in order to provide the lord with income, clothes, and amusements. They are persecuted with fire, looting and the sword; they are thrown into prison and irons and then forced to buy themselves free or they are killed violently by starvation and exposed to all kinds of torture . . . The poor scream, the widows weep, the orphans sigh, the tortured spill their blood.'

Serfdom was one of the most sombre aspects of medieval feudalism. It had developed out of the system of captivity at war under which the captives and their offspring were the property of the victorious lord and in the Middle Ages it became an accepted institution. Serfdom could be decreed as punishment, for instance if the peasant could not pay his rent. At times, however, the poor or debtors voluntarily became serfs in order not to starve. In addition many peasants became serfs simply as a result of the coercion of a noble lord who could then sell them like objects or cattle. A document dating from 1333 describes this: 'I, Conrad the Lord High Steward of Urach, Knight, hereby make known and make public to all those who read, see or hear this letter, that I have given to the Honourable ecclesiastical Lord, the Abbot and the Convent of Lorch Monastery, the two women Agnes and her sister Mahilt, blessed daughters of Degan Reinbolt, and any child that may be born of them, for three pounds of farthings; I have received this [fee] from him, which I confirm by this letter, sealed with my seal which is attached to it. This letter was written in the year 1333 counting from the Birth of Christ.'

Today it is difficult to imagine the dreadful life of the 'poor people', as the peasants were officially called until the 17th century, a life which was made almost unbearable by the burden of dues, compulsory labour and taxes, from the tithe to rents of hens and eggs. The situation of the peasants seemed hopeless. But this firmly entrenched social system based on an agricultural economy was severely shaken by the rise of the towns.

Most of the Roman towns were destroyed during the migration of nations or fell into ruin since they were alien to the rural Germans. The historian Tacitus c. 120 A.D.) wrote in his 'Germania': 'The Germanic tribes do not, as we know, live in towns; they cannot even tolerate living in enclosed places.' Only those towns in which bishops established sees survived. There was a papal decree that bishops had to reside in towns. Examples of Roman citadels or towns which became episcopal sees in the German-speaking territory are Constance, Augsburg, Cologne, Aachen, Trier, Mainz, Worms, Speyer, Strasbourg, Basle and Zurich. These 'civitates', (from the Latin 'cives' = citizen), as the episcopal towns were known, consisted of the dwellings of the bishop's retinue and his secular retainers. But they were also the dwelling

133

place of peasants and craftsmen and the sites of the first markets and craft activities.

Originally the episcopal towns were not fortified. But in the 9th century the Normans raided the coasts and river valleys of the Kingdom of the Franks and for the next two centuries they looted the villages and towns all the way from England down to Sicily. This was a gravated by the advance of the Arabs from the South to France and the invasions of the Slavs, Avars and Hungarians, some of whom penetrated as far as eastern France, where Basle, for instance, was stormed and destroyed by the Hungarians in 917. These warlike raids finally led to the construction of town fortifications, usually defensive walls. It was the same reason that had caused the nobility to build so many castles in the 10th century; and the German kings (e.g. Henry I) also built places of refuge and fortresses. This created a fortified system of defence which eventually managed to halt the raids of the invaders. During the period of peace which then began, economic life revived again. The 'civitates' and the markets near the palatines and royal courts were not towns in the economic, and certainly not in the legal sense, since the inhabitants did not govern themselves nor did they have equal rights. At that time town dwellers had exactly the same legal status as the country folk, that is to say, they were serfs of the municipal lord. They could not leave the town without the consent of the lord – the king, bishop, abbot or secular prince. The serf could neither sell nor mortgage the place where he resided because it belonged to the lord, as did all his property. That is why even the town dweller had to arrange that on his death the best head of cattle was given to his lord, or if he had no cattle, the best piece of clothing. But these early towns already embodied the rudiments of a new social order whose origins lie in the revival of foreign trade.

After the Mediterranean had been divided up into two zones of influence in the 7th century with the advance of the Arabs, and Europe finally lost much of that great trading area of Roman times, the emporium between Asia, Africa and Europe, trade with the distant countries of the East also came to a stop. Not until the 9th century did new trade contacts develop with the Arabs of the East, as we learn from finds of Arab silver coins in Scandinavia and Russia. The economic life of Antiquity had survived in the Byzantine Empire, however, and in the 10th century Constantinople was the most important trading town in the known world of the time. Its outpost in Western Europe was Venice, which lived only from trade. Amalfi also began to trade with Constantinople early on until it fell under Norman rule in 1070. With the transfer of the seat of the Fatimids from Kairouan in Tunisia to Cairo at the end of the 10th century, the Italian coastal towns adopted a much more expansive trade policy. In 975 a fleet of Byzantine and Pisan ships attacked the Arab town of Messina in Sicily and in 1016 Pisan and Genoan forces advanced to Corsica and Sardinia. These towns became early centres of the reviving trade. The trade routes led from there over the Alpine passes in the north and later through Provence to northern France and Flanders. Another trade route ran from Constantinople via Kiev to Novgorod, thence to the Baltic and to England and Flanders. Here the Swedish Vikings, the Varangians, traded with Constantinople and above all with the Asian Moslems. From the 9th century on the Swedish Varangians built up the so-called Kingdom of Kiev and controlled the Volga and the Dniepr, 'the route from the Varangians to the Greeks'. But in around 1050 the Varangian trade with Byzantium and the Arabs dried up again. Other important medieval trade routes led from Rome through the valley of the Rhône to York; from northern Italy to Santiago de Compostela in north-western Spain; from Cordoba in southern Spain via the valley of the Rhône, Verdun, Mainz, Regensburg, Prague, Krakow, Przemysl to Kiev; along the Danube from

134

73–75 Carcassonne, Aude (the Gallo-Roman town of Carcaso) was an episcopal see from the 4th century, belonged to the kingdom of the Visigoths from 418, was taken by the Arabs in 724 and conquered by the Franks in 725. It was a hill castle of the Albigensians at one stage. When Carcassonne surrendered to Simon de Montfort in 1209, the town became a Capetian base in southern France and a bastion of the church during the persecution of the heretic Albigensians. The old, upper town on a steeply sloping rise is surrounded by two huge enclosing walls with 53 towers (12th and 13th centuries). It had some 10 dynastic towers which served as residences for the various noble families. All in all Carcassonne is the mightiest walled castle of medieval Europe. Restored by Viollet-le-Duc in the 19th century, it now offers a convincing picture of a medieval, southern French fortified town.

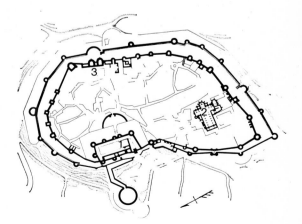

Carcassonne, ground plan
1 Castle
2 Cathedral
3 Porte Narbonnaise

Regensburg to Constantinople; from the Mediterranean ports of Barcelona, Narbonne, Genoa, Pisa, Amalfi and Venice to Constantinople, Tunis, Alexandria and Tyre on the Syrian coast.

Precious fabrics, silks, skins, jewellery, weapons, metal, corn, wine, spices, salt and Eastern luxury goods and slaves – arrived in the central European towns along many of these trade routes. For instance, it is written in a Russian chronicle: 'In that year [969] Sviatoslav wanted to transfer his capital from Kiev to Pereiaslavec [on the Danube]. In that town there was an accumulation of everything: the gold of the Greeks, precious fabrics, wines and various

135

fruits, silver and horses from Bohemia and Hungary, leather and wax, honey and slaves from Russia.' According to the report of an Arab traveller Ibn-Jakub, Prague was one of the biggest slave markets in Europe. Usually serfs were sold to Jewish traders by their (Christian) masters who then resold them inside and outside Europe. Another Arab, a certain Masudi, tells of the fur trade in the 10th century: 'The area of the Burta [a tribe of Islamic Volga-Bulgarians] exports the furs of the black fox, the most sought-after and expensive fur. The black fox is the luxury fur of the princes of the non-Arab peoples, and it is exported as far as the regions of Derbent and Barda, to Chorosan and Chvarezm, where the furs are treated. But they also go to the north, to the Slav countries, for the Burta live not far from the northern territories. From the Slav areas the goods are then taken to all the lands of the Franks and to the western lands of the Moslems.'

The merchants who were engaged in trade with far countries formed a social group in themselves. They included very many Jews, since the Jews found support wherever there were Jewish communities and were the only non-Mohammedans to be allowed to travel the countries of Islam freely. The foreign traders sailed the seas, used the waterways of the rivers and crossed the whole of Europe with their covered wagons or simply with mules. The occupation of the merchant is described by the Anglo-Saxon Aelfryc in *c.* 1000 in the following words: 'I load my wares in my ship, travel over the sea, sell my cargo and buy products which one cannot find in England. I bring them to you here.'

Originally the merchants were not tied to any town or village and were not in bondage to any lord. They were free individuals and did not come under jurisdiction of the municipal lords. They were often exempt from military and labour services and from tributes and were directly subordinate to the king (which is why they were called 'royal merchants'), the county court and market law. The municipal lord had no claim to their property and they only had to pay agreed duties to enable them to offer their wares on the market. These foreign traders founded settlements outside the town walls where they stored their merchandise. They fortified their depots with palisades, walls and ditches. Eventually the merchants' quarters ('portus', 'vicus', 'borgus', hence French 'bourg', English 'burh' and 'boroughs'; Frankish 'wik') also became the place of residence of settled merchants, specialized craftsmen, money-changers and money-lenders, the callings which developed around trade. Jews settled here too since they did not need to try to dodge the Christian veto on levying interest as the Christians did. During the 'natural' economy period, the charging of interest on a loan (usury) had seemed to conflict with the Christian commandment to love thy neighbour. Payment was to be given only for work actually done, which is why the church forbade charging interest. This veto was often avoided by the purchase of an annuity: the money-lender bought an annuity, an annual interest, which the debtor had to pay until the debt was paid off. In the 'burgi' or 'suburbia' which were sometimes connected with the town proper (the 'urbs') by a wall from the 10th century on, a new sense of community gradually grew up among the inhabitants. The merchants joined into guilds for greater protection and mutual aid and began to organize various forms of community life and to make arrangements to protect their freedom. This necessarily engendered conflicts with the lord which finally led to the creation of communes which gradually wrested from the lords their sovereign rights over the court, police, taxes, minting, etc.

The word 'burgensis', burgess, first appears around the year 1000 to denote the inhabitant of a town. That was probably the time when the difference between the legal status of the rural dweller and the town dweller evolved. The towns obtained charters of liberties. The earliest Italian town charter was 75

138

given to Genoa in 958, and released the town from the authority of the royal representative. The first charters of several northern Spanish (Christian) towns also date to that time. North of the Alps the first coinage and market privileges were conferred after the opening of trade over the Alpine passes. As early as 947 Otto I had granted the Abbey of St Gall market and coinage privileges for Rorschach. The Abbey of Reichenau obtained these rights in 998 for Allensbach from Otto III. And in 1045 Emperor Henry II conferred coinage rights on the lord of Schaffhausen, Eberhard III von Nellenburg, an indication that the Rhine was opened to shipping. Thus the conferral of privileges on the towns marks the expansion of trade.

To the extent that trade expanded, especially after the crusades, it became easier for the towns to obtain pirvileges because the lords of the towns rightly expected to gain considerable revenue by levying duties and taxes. The privileges which were granted to the towns throughout Europe, from England to Italy and from Spain and France to the Slavic borders, from the mid-11th century on embodied much the same rights: inviolability of the home, the abolition of the legal duel, the right of the burgesses to submit to no jurisdiction other than that of their town. In addition the burgesses were usually granted freedom of trade and were exempt from duties if they married foreigners and from succession duties, etc. A change in property law gave the burgesses the right of ownership of land if they paid the landowner a sum of twenty times the annual ground rent. From the 12th century on this produced towns in the legal sense; their inhabitants also had a different, freer legal status than the country dwellers most of whom remained serfs and vassals. Among the many privileges of the burgess, the most important was the 'privilegium de non evocando', which meant that the burgess could only be summoned before the town court; the town thus acquired its own area of jurisdiction. Under the principle that 'town air liberates', serfs and vassals who lived in a town for one year without the lord demanding their return became free; in the same way the marriage of a burgess and a female serf gave the serf freedom. Equality under the law and autonomy became the main characteristics of urban life. The towns thus acquired their own historic liberties which were conferred in turn on new towns as and when they were founded. The new penal code was generally stricter than the old one and aimed chiefly at punishing breaches of the peace and of the business code, sometimes by death. The Bern manifesto of 1218, which is mainly based on the law of the city of Cologne, states the following: 'He who kills within the context of the aims and the peace of the town shall be decapitated without question. If he wounds in a spirit of anger, he shall forfeit his hand. If the accused should escape and is not captured and, after being summoned three times, does not appear before the court, he shall be deemed to have admitted his fault and convicted himself. Then the mayor and the council and all the burgesses shall demolish his house entirely and leave the ruins untouched on the site for a year and a day. At the end of the year his heirs may build it up again if they so wish and freely own it; first, however, they must pay the judge three pounds. But if the accused should later return at any time to the town and be caught, he shall suffer the same punishment as though he had been captured on the first day.'

A new system of taxation evolved which was graded according to the wealth of the burgess, unlike the old uniform per capita tax. As the towns became autonomous, so urban authorities came into being, the most important of which was the town council. Officials were eligible and removable – in contrast to the lifelong and usually still hereditary feudal law. To the prestige ensured by 'high birth' now came the recognition of achievement.

76 Carcassonne, Aude: 'Porte Narbonnaise', the gate through which the road led to Narbonne, is the main gate of the town. Its two towers are 82 ft high. The front gate was restored in the 19th century and presumably does not correspond exactly to the original gate.

140

77 Carcassonne, Aude: 'Porte Narbonnaise' with the statue of the Virgin over the entrance. The long embrasures and narrow vertical loopholes in the tower walls made it possible effectively to defend the entrance, which was of course closed in times of attack.

Fortified Towns in Southern France and Italy

Many of the towns and villages of southern France and Italy represent a special form of medieval defensive and military complex. Instead of individual castles, it is the whole town that is fortified.

Fortified towns had existed in southern France since Roman times and most of the medieval towns were built inside the walls of Roman towns (a good example is Nîmes). In contrast to northern France, here and in Italy the landlords preferred to live in the towns, which they protected with thick walls, rather than in free-standing rural fortresses. The result was that in southern France and in Italy the town developed along different lines from its counterpart in northern Europe. In the north the town was a residential community of burgesses who could assert themselves *vis à vis* the nobility. The inhabitants earned their living from crafts and trade, which is why it was important for the towns to be situated on trade routes. As we have seen the boom in trade and crafts enabled many northern towns to acquire a high degree of autonomy and self-government.

The aspect of the northern European town was determined by its imposing

142

civic houses, town halls, guild houses, etc. Things were different in southern France and Italy. There the feudal lords and the patricians were mainly concerned with the effective defence of their possessions and their authority. Only the Mediterranean ports (Marseille, Narbonne, Montpellier) were to some extent an exception, but Mediterranean trade came to an end there in the 14th century. The southern towns were what is called 'consular towns', i.e., they were ruled by annually elected consuls; below them came the council and the town meeting which were made up almost entirely of nobles, however. Between 1145 and 1155 the consulate of Arles, for instance, consisted of twelve consuls four of whom were knights, four patricians of the town, two market representatives and two from the suburb of Borriano. During this period the Archbishop of Arles granted the town limited self-government in order to guarantee peace: 'This consulate personifies peace, the restoration of the good old days and the reform of society. The churches, monasteries and all sacred places dedicated to God, the roads and public ways, the waters and the land, over all these peace shall reign. Peace will be sworn for a period of fifty years and every five years strangers and new arrivals shall swear to keep the peace. In this way the consulate will be renewed and preserved; the entire community which is thus held intact for the service of God and the public good will continue to prosper, thanks to the intercession of the archbishop . . . If a dispute should arise in the town, no slinger or archer, armed with stone or bow, may attack any person within the town or settlement. And no stranger may enter the community except at the wish and with the consent of the bishop and all the consuls.' Pacts of peace of this kind between the lord and the burgesses often put a stop to townsmen's attempts to gain greater self-government. In general it is true to say that the medieval French towns (communes in the north, consular towns in the south) never gained the kind of independence enjoyed by the German imperial towns, perhaps largely because of the strength of the central royal power. The southern French towns which had grown out of Roman fortified towns and indigenous fortified villages were interested less in trade routes than in good defensive positions when choosing the geographical location of a town, so that the towns were often situated by the bend of a river or on a hill. Below are a few characteristic examples of such fortified towns.

A typical fortified hill town of southern France is Cordes on the Tarn (Ill. 72). The Cathedral of St Michel rises on the northern spur of a long ridge while the houses huddle together on the slopes. This small town, which now has only some 1000 inhabitants, developed out of the 'bastide' (blockhouse of a nobleman) founded in 1222 by the count of Toulouse, Raymond VII. As a result of the population growth in the 14th century the town spread further down to the foot of the hill. It was almost impregnable thanks to a complicated system of defensive walls, the foundations of the houses which reached to the bottom of the slope, the houses themselves, and the layout of the streets, gates and steps.

Carcassonne (Ills. 73–78) is situated in the middle of the Languedoc on the Aude. The old town was built on a bluff sloping down steeply on all sides. It is an amalgam of mainly Romanesque and Gothic buildings which were restored by Viollet-le-Duc in the 19th century, so that today we have an almost complete picture of this medieval town. The oldest buildings date from the 6th century, the period of the Tolosan Visigothic kingdom (hence the name of the capital, Toulouse). The medieval town was protected by double castle walls the inner wall of which was erected at the end of the 12th century, the outer in the 13th under St Louis when Carcassonne became an important royal base in southern France. The enormous town walls were reinforced by a total of 53 towers which projected outward over the walls so that the attackers who had reached close up to the walls could be fought off from the flank. Since it was

78 Carcassonne, Aude. The castle of Carcassonne dates from the first half of the 12th century and occupies a large area of the fortified town. It is situated by the inner city wall and was designed to reinforce the northwest flank; but it could also be defended independently of the fortified town. A wide moat surrounds the strong castle walls.

79

79 Aigues-Mortes, Gard. The town and harbour were built by Louis IX in the mid-13th century as an arms depot, disembarkation harbour and supply depot for his crusades and protected by a wall. The town moats have been filled in again now so that the walls look lower than they in fact were at the time.

80 Aigues-Mortes, Gard. View of the wall-walk on the city walls and the 'Tour de Constance'. The name probably derives from that of an earlier tower which Raymond V of St Gilles, Count of Toulouse, built in the 12th century and is said to have called after his wife, the daughter of the French king Louis VI. The 98 ft tower is surmounted on the southern side by a 32 ft small tower also dating from the 13th century. The wrought-iron lantern is of a later date. Originally the tower was crenellated; the present flat top, rounded off on the outside, was only built when it was converted into a state prison in the 17th century. The tower was surrounded by a wet moat round its base which measured 72 ft in diameter, with walls 20 ft thick; it served as the king's residential tower and as a watch-tower which could give warning of danger to the interior of the country.

81

81 *Aigues-Mortes, Gard. Roads run between the wall and the town (Ill. 80) and wide steps lead up to the angle towers and gate towers so that troops could be moved rapidly from one area of attack to another without difficulty.*

82 *Aigues-Mortes, Gard. View from the 'Tower of Constance' ('Tour de Constance') built by St Louis to protect the harbour. It is separated from the town by a wet moat and forms a fortress in its own right. St Louis is said to have embarked straight from this tower into the crusader ship.*

always possible that individual towers might fall into the hands of the attackers, the towers were not equipped with any fixed armature. Some ten of these towers once served as the residences of various noble families. The imposing castle (Ill. 78) of the counts of Carcassonne is adjacent to the inner wall. It was designed to strengthen the north-western flank but could also withstand heavy attacks independently of the other town fortifications. It was built in the 12th century. A wide moat surrounds the castle wall.

One of the most interesting southern French towns is Aigues-Mortes (Ills. 79–83). Until the 13th century the French crown owned no Mediterranean ports. But between 1240 and 1248 St Louis acquired land on the bay of Eaux-Mortes, at the mouth of the so-called Lesser Rhône, from the monastery Psalmodi. Here a port was built from which the king, together with his brothers Charles of Anjou and Alphonse of Poitiers, set sail for the Sixth Crusade in 1248. This crusade was unsuccessful for the Christians and in fact the king and his entire army were captured during the march on Cairo in 1250 and only released against a large ransom. Louis IX built the 30 m high tower, the 'Tour de Constance' (Ills. 80, 82), to defend this harbour and as his residence. It is built like a keep and stands like a watchman in front of the later

148

83 Aigues-Mortes, Gard. The 'Porte de la Reine', the queen's gate, dating from the mid-13th century, clearly illustrates the solid forces of the fortifications of this newly founded town which were not built up on any earlier defensive structures. The gateways were protected by doors, portcullises and embrasures and flanked by two towers which could only be entered from the wall-walk. The two storeys of the towers are connected by a spiral stairway. Archers could aim down at the area in front of the entrance from long, narrow loopholes. The upper storeys of the towers are linked above the entrance by a room from which the portcullises could be operated and missiles projected through the embrasures in the gatehouse. These gatehouses, constructed according to very skilful military techniques, serve as small fortresses in their own right.

84 *Albi, Tarn. The fortified Cathedral of Albi, the foundation stone of which was laid by Bishop Bernard de Castané in 1282, towers over the town from which the Albigensians derive their name. This fortified church was probably constructed because of the persecution of the heretic Albigensians at the end of the Albigensian Wars.*

town wall. It was an ideal observation and warning tower and its beacon could warn remote villages and towns of any danger approaching from the sea. In the second half of the 13th century a harbour town gradually came into being, which Philip III the Bold began to fortify with a vast city wall. Soon this enterprise proved too expensive, however, so in 1272 the king had it financed by a Genoese financier. Guillaume Boccanegra was to obtain a half share in the ownership of town and harbour against sharing half the costs with the king. But he died only two years later and his heirs dissolved the contract. Finally the building work was completed under Philip IV the Fair (1285–1314), probably still in the 13th century. However, the fairway began to silt up by the 14th century and the port became unusable.

Since the town fortifications did not have to take account of any existing settlement they could be built purely according to defensive requirements. They are as simple and effective as can be and without doubt represent the most advanced defensive system of the second half of the 14th century. The mighty wall some 11 m high is based on an almost regular rectangle and transforms the entire town into a fortress. The corners and five main gates are protected by round towers. The wall is built of irregular sized large, squared stone. Partially preserved battements top the wall and the merlons are slit with long, narrow loopholes widening towards the interior to enlarge the field of fire. Hot liquids and projectiles could be poured or thrown down on any attackers who had advanced up to the wall from machicolations and shafts which may also have served as latrines. There are also a number of loopholes in the wall below the battlements and behind them are shooting niches for two people. The gates (Ill. 83) were protected by iron doors, portcullises and machicolations. They were further secured by two projecting round towers

85 San Gimignano. In the 13th and 14th centuries this lovely little medieval town in Tuscany had some 70 dynastic towers in which the patrician families who were usually quarrelling with each other lived. Today only 13 towers survive yet they give the town its characteristic aspect.

which could only be reached from the wall-walk. The two floors of the towers were connected by a spiral stairway. Attackers near the entrance could be shot at from embrasures. There are windows facing the town, although the windows on the outside of the wall date from a later period. The upper storeys of the towers are connected above the entrance by a room from which the defenders could work the portcullises and the pouring holes inside the entrance. The militarily very skilful entrances act as small fortresses in themselves within the general defensive system of the town. The secondary gates are protected in similar fashion. A road (Ill. 80) runs from the walls to the town so that troops could be shifted from one area of attack to another quickly and smoothly. For the same reason wide steps lead up to the corner towers and gates (Ill. 81). The wall-walk is also rather wide (*c.* 2·50 m) so that a large number of defenders could change position rapidly (Ills. 79, 80).

Fortified churches often played an important part in this kind of fortified town. Even from the outside they bear some resemblance to castles. Especially in rural areas, they were built on a rise dominating the countryside. The building was of solid stone with a tower and often both were surrounded by a wall. This made it easy to convert the church into a fortress where the local people could seek refuge in times of war. Like many of the monasteries, the churches were often fortified just as strongly as castles, with moats, drawbridge, watchtowers and walls. There were military churches throughout Europe in the Middle Ages. Very impressive buildings are found in southern France, sometimes forming part of the overall defensive system of the town. The fortified church was rarely built in the centre of the town but more often on the edge, close to the town wall or even connected with it directly (Toulouse, Carcassonne, Cahors, Bordeaux). With the expansion of the town in later times the churches increasingly became the focal point of the town. Where the fortified churches had been designed as such originally, they were built on the most inaccessible sites, on steep cliffs, hilltops, etc., which gave them a key role in the defence of fortified towns and villages.

One of the most impressive fortress-churches of southern France is the cathedral of Albi (Ill. 84). Its foundation stone was laid by Bishop Bernard de Castane in 1282. Its construction was perhaps bound up with the end of the Albigensian wars during which the heretic movement of the Cathars or Albigensians (from their castle of Albi) was overcome, large areas of southern

153

France including Languedoc were brought under the Capetian king (Treaty of Paris, 1229), and the ancient Provencal culture was destroyed. This church stands as a bastion defending the Christian orthodoxy of the expansive North and the Catholic church against the religious, cultural and political movements for independence of the South.

In Italy the ancient towns were never destroyed as completely as north of the Alps. Bishops established their sees in many former Roman towns, and after the decline of the power of the state they upheld secular order in addition to performing their ecclesiastical functions. These early episcopal towns were called 'civitates' – hence the term 'cite', or 'city', which remained when the towns later expanded. With the revival of trade, at first mainly in the seaboard towns of Venice, Amalfi, Pisa and Genoa, and later also in the inland towns of Lombardy and Tuscany (Milan, Pavia, Florence, etc), powerful urban communes developed in Italy which acquired a leading position in European commerce and credit financing. They were usually situated on the site of ancient Roman or Etruscan settlements, parts of which, such as the town

86   Orvieto. The town of Orvieto, situated 650 ft above the foot of the valley in an outstanding position, is a well-preserved example of the medieval town. There was a settlement here as early as Etruscan times although it was destroyed by the Romans in 280 B.C. Later the Romans rebuilt it and called it 'Urbs Vetus' (Old Town), from which it derives its present name. In the 12th century the town was a centre of the Guelfs and gave refuge to the popes on several occasions. Left of centre stands the famous cathedral, one of the most beautiful churches in Italy, begun in 1290 and completed in the Gothic style in the 14th century.

154

walls or the amphitheatre, had survived and could be adapted to new purposes. With the growth of trade the towns also acquired greater autonomy. In Amalfi and Venice the burgesses could elect their own doge, the chief magistrate, as early as the 10th century. But whereas in Flanders, northern Germany or northern France the nobility lived in castles outside the town, in the south they took part in building up the towns and in trade. In Italy the state privileges (coinage, customs, courts) were in the hands of individual noble families. This association of bourgeoisie and nobility created an effective bond between military skill and the financial ability which was to prove more important in the long term. The urban nobility also made its mark on the Italian towns in architectural terms. Even today the aspect of many central Italian towns is determined by the dynastic towers in which the noble and patrician families once lived.

A typical example is the little town of San Gimignano (Ill. 85) in Tuscany, between Florence and Siena. It grew up in the 10th century round a castle on a hill 324 m high which gives a lovely view over the Tuscan landscape. In the

155

13th and 14th centuries San Gimignano was a flourishing free commune. Today 13 dynastic towers of the nobility still survive: at one time there were 70, the dwellings of the powerful noble families of the town, like the Salvucci and the Ardinghelli. The towers were used as homes and as defensive towers in times of war or during the bitter feuds between the families for domination of the town.

The fortified hill towns and villages give the medieval landscapes of Tuscany and Umbria their peculiar character. Even today their defensive character remains clearly recognizable. They developed in the confused period between the decline of the Western Roman Empire, when the power of the state gradually dwindled, and the Middle Ages, although the present aspect of these settlements with their old houses and fortifications does not go back before the 11th century. It is easy to understand the reasons for the difficult and laborious construction of these towns and villages on hills. The power of the state to protect the people had disappeared. Bands of looters now traversed the country and foreign peoples invaded Italy in search of conquest or merely of plunder. At the same time the lowlands had often become almost uninhabitable since the old drainage systems had fallen into ruin and the land was gradually turning to swamp again. That is why the trade routes ran across the hill passes, which involved major detours but offered the only accessible passage: the old, straight trade routes of the Romans had long since fallen into disrepair. The lay-out of these hill towns depended entirely on the lie of the land for it was not possible to build according to a systematic plan as in the case of the old Roman towns or the medieval towns which had been built on the plains – as many drivers now discover to their despair. The construction of the town according to the condition of the terrain at times also affected its social and political structure. For instance the political organization of Siena in the Middle Ages corresponded to the situation of the town on three hills. It had three districts which elected the 'Council of Nine' that guided the destinies of the town from 1282 to 1352.

The exposed, impregnable and dominant position of the medieval hill towns is well illustrated by Orvieto in Umbria (Ill. 86). This town is located on a free-standing volcanic hill which rises 200 m above the bottom of the valley. Orvieto stands on the site of the old Etruscan Volsinii which was destroyed by the Romans in 280 B.C. but later rebuilt by them and given the name 'Urbs Vetus' (Old Town) whence its present name derives. In the 12th century Orvieto was the centre of the Guelfs, the followers of the pope and advocates of the freedom of towns who since 1212 had been at war with the Ghibellines (named after the Swabian town of Waiblingen), who supported the German emperor. This struggle continued for centuries. The town also served as a refuge for the popes on several occasions.

The cathedral rises from narrow, medieval alleys. It is one of the most beautiful of Italian churches and was begun in 1290 in the Romanesque style and completed in the Gothic style in the 14th century. The façade with its magnificent mosaic and sculptural decoration is rightly famous. Pope Urban IV had this splendid church built to the glory of the 'Miracle of Bolsena'. The story goes that on his journey from Prague to Rome in 1263 a Bohemian priest was reading the mass in Bolsena. But he doubted the doctrine of the transubstantiation, the dogma of the transformation of the substance of bread and wine into the flesh and blood of Christ. During the transubstantiation the host began to bleed, ridding the pious man of his doubts. Urban IV instituted Corpus Christi day, which has been Italy's main religious feast day since that time, in memory of this miracle.

With the collapse of the German imperial power in Italy the Italian towns gained their full independence. In their struggle against the emperor, the northern Italian towns had formed federations which gave Emperor

Frederick I Barbarossa (1152–1190) bitter experience of their military capacity. Gradually genuine city-states formed which were constantly in dispute with one another besides being torn apart by internal strife. Nevertheless trade and the arts flourished, spurred on by competition between the towns. By the end of the 14th century Florence had become the leading town of Tuscany. In 1405 it gained sovereignty over Pisa and in 1421 it bought the port of Leghorn from the Genoese. After 1434 Florence was completely under the influence of the powerful banker Cosimo de' Medici who brought the most important artists and scholars of his time to the city and founded the Platonic Academy. This was the time when Brunelleschi and Michelangelo built the great cathedral dome and the Medici Palace. In 1531 the Medici became dukes of Florence and in 1569 grand dukes of Tuscany. The family did not die out until 1737.

In southern Tuscany Siena was growing increasingly powerful thanks to its trade and its credit business. It was Sienese bankers who financed the French crusaders. Today the wealth of this town in the Middle Ages can be retraced in its magnificent buildings, including the huge cathedral, one of the most beautiful Gothic churches in Italy. Originally the building was to have been the nave of an even more enormous church but this project proved rather too ambitious and was eventually abandoned. The Campo with the glorious Palazzo Publicco is one of the loveliest medieval squares in Italy. For a long time this mighty rival of Florence managed to avoid the influence of the Medici town but it had to surrender in 1577. The city-state of Genoa extended over wide areas of the Riviera and Corsica until in 1379 it finally came under Venice after almost a century of quarrels.

During the Fourth Crusade Venice managed to conquer Constantinople in 1204 thereby destroying the economic and political predominance of the Byzantine Empire in the Eastern Mediterranean. Subsequently it built up its own vast colonial empire on the Adriatic and the Eastern Mediterranean. In northern Italy its territory ('Terra ferma') extended from Venice to Padua and from Verona to Bergamo. It was ruled by a doge elected for life and controlled by the Council of Ten. Politically and socially it was relatively stable thanks to the strong and well-organized police system. With the discovery of America in 1492 this mighty republic gradually began to decline since world trade now followed new directions.

Milan was the leading Lombard town. Like Venice it was completely dominated by the aristocracy. The feuds between the Della Torre and Visconti families were finally resolved in favour of the Visconti in 1310 with the support of the German emperor. The most important ruler was Giangaleazzo Visconti (1351–1402), the most powerful Italian prince of his time. He conquered Verona, then Padua, Bologna, Pisa, Siena and Perugia. In fact he was about to appoint himself king of Italy when he died suddenly before the conquest of Florence. Under the rule of Giangaleazzo Visconti, trade, the arts and scholarship flourished in Milan. It was he who ordered the construction of Milan Cathedral, the largest Gothic church it Italy.

The economic power of the towns was reflected clearly in their political power. Their social structure in particular, differed radically from that of feudal society. The freedom of the towns in the late Middle Ages was the basis for the growth of the modern bourgeoisie. For a new privileged class, distinct from the rural inahbitants, and called the 'Third Estate' had taken its place in the towns beside the nobility and the church, to the angry astonishment of the existing rulers. The Cistercian abbot, Bishop Otto of Freising (1111–1158), author of a historical and philosophical treatise on Italian towns, wrote: '[The emperor], to whom they had to show spontaneous reverence and submission, is hardly if ever received with respect and even his commands in the name of the sacredness of the law are not greeted with obedience unless the people are made to feel his power by the pressure of the host of his great army.'

87

87, 88 *Nuremberg. The castle of Nuremberg is first mentioned in documents in 1050 when Emperor Henry III held court here. It formed part of a complex of fortifications in front of the eastern border hills. Between 1070 and 1571 all the German emperors stayed in the imperial castle at least once. In the Golden Bull of 1356, Charles IV decreed that every elected German king must hold his first imperial diet in Nuremberg. The castle consists of two main structures: the imperial castle in the west and the burgrave's castle with remains of the Salian royal castle (pentagonal tower), together with the defensive structures of the town. The imperial castle was built by the Hohenstaufen king Conrad III in the 12th century (and extended until the 16th century) after the old Salian castle was destroyed by Duke Henry of Bavaria in 1130. The rebuilt old castle was henceforth used as the residence of the burgraves. Ill. 88 shows the 'Sinwell Tower' ('sinwell' = round), the watchtower of the imperial castle dating from the 12th century. The tent roof surmounted by a helm-roofed superstructure dates from c. 1560. The tower stands on a natural rock and was designed to protect the eastern flank which was the point of attack of the castle.*

German towns

As in Italy, the nobility in the south German and Swiss towns often played a part in the construction, administration and government of the towns. As in Italy too, dynastic towers were built in Regensburg, Schaffhausen, Basle and Zurich: 'They are situated at street intersections or on the walls of earlier fortifications, stone structures, in the centre of the wooden town which therefore look all the more powerful, eclipsing the alleys with their defiant mass', as the historian of the town of Basle describes them. So it is not surprising to find nobles on the council of many 13th-century southern German towns together with merchants.

All the burgesses were in fact equal under the law but social and political power was usually in the hands of a small group of rich bourgeois families, the patricians: foreign traders ('mercatores'), 'ministeriales' and the free landowners. In Germany the export traders largely determined the fate of the towns of Cologne, Regensburg, Vienna, Aachen, Augsburg, Ulm, Würzburg, Nuremberg, Dortmund, Erfurt, Halle, Leipzig, Bremen, Hamburg, Lüdbeck, etc. The 'ministriales' were powerful in Worms, Strasbourg, Trier and Zurich. The landowners had great influence in the town councils of Soest, Osnabrück, Nuremberg and Munich.

These conditions were graphically described in *c.* 1280 by the knight Philip of Beaumanoir, steward of the French King in Clermont-de-l'Oise: 'We see several good towns in which the poor and the middle class have no share in the municipal administration; the rich keep everything in their hands for they want no communion with those who are too poor or of low birth. This year one of them is mayor, juryman or tax collector, next year it is his brother, nephew or close relative . . . Often the rich who rule the town tax themselves and their relatives lower than they should so that later they too will be expempted and thus all the taxes tend to oppress the poor.'

With the economic boom of the towns, a third group now developed whose increasing economic importance also led it to demand a say in political matters: the artisans who had long been excluded from the town council. By the 14th century the aristocratic classes (urban nobility and merchants who had become rich) were faced in several towns by the power of the guilds and council seats were allocated to the guilds of artisans and shopkeepers. These guilds were coercive cooperative associations which kept watch over the artisans' work, the entire production process, quality, wages and prices. Only guild members could pursue a craft in their town. In the guild-towns the guilds were ruled by the council which managed the entire economy of the town taking account of the interests of its burgesses and even organizing social security facilities for them (almshouses and hospitals).

In the 12th century the Hohenstaufen kings began to protect their family property by founding new towns, which also brought the advantage of better and more systematic administration. The Hohenstaufen crown estates were scattered throughout the empire; the largest connected areas of land lay in Alsace, Swabia and eastern Franconia, which is why most of the new towns were built in those areas. Emperor Frederick I Barbarossa renounced the feudal system and transferred the administration to royal officials who could be deposed. Hereditary stewards gradually gave way in the royal towns to mayors and bailiffs. Frederick II greatly strengthened the royal power by acquiring church fiefs at the election of bishops and abbots. For it was important to a new town who exercized the sovereign rights in the respective area, but less important whom the land belonged to. So the acquisition of church domains by the king was a favourite means of protecting his sovereignty.

The new towns were planned in accordance with economic, trade and

89 Nuremberg. View of the 'Heathen's Tower' ('Heidenturm') which fronts the double chapel, the most important element of the castle. Both date from the late 12th century and are thus the oldest parts of the imperial castle. The 'Heathen's Tower' derives its names from the Romanesque stone figures on the east façade, of which two rows of lions and seated figures still survive. The other figurative sculptures were destroyed before Charles V's visit in 1520 as 'sundry heathen bosses and images'. It is possible that they represent the founders of the Bamberg episcopal see, Henry II and his wife Kunigunde.

90 *Nuremberg. View from the castle and the 'Heathen's Tower' onto the town. Immediately to the left of the 'Heathen's Tower' in the illustration is the 13th-century 'Tiergärtnerturm' ('Park-keeper's Gate-house') which forms part of the city wall. Diagonally opposite stands Dürer's house, dating from the mid-15th century, which the painter bought in 1509. The round tower further back is the 'Neutor' (New Gate) of 1559.*

political factors. We have already mentioned that the administration of crown land gave rise to certain local necessities. In addition there was the need to protect the roads, the intersections of busy trade routes, the river crossings and the waterways. That is why the new towns were still fortified. Often the castle and the town together formed an effective defensive system, as in Friedberg in Hessen, Wetzlar, Reutlingen and Nuremberg. Nuremberg (Ills. 87–90) was first mentioned in 1050 when Emperor Henry III held court here. In order to strengthen the royal power in Eastern Franconia and to protect the border against Bohemia he founded a castle in 1040/41 close to the old royal court of Fürth on a hill above the Pegnitz. The outhouses were used for reinforcements during the raids against the Bohemian duke Bratislav. Nuremberg was also the meeting place of the roads from Bavaria, Franconia, Swabia and Bohemia. Soon this well-situated market and trading town was settled by merchants who obtained the same privileges there as in other towns. The town grew quickly, dividing into two parts, the settlement at the foot of the castle round the church of Sebaldus and the settlement on the other bank of the Pegnitz round the main church of St Lorenz. The two parts were not united until *c*. 1320. The rapidly growing town was encircled three times with a town wall, the last of which was built in 1377 and is 1 m thick and 7–8 m high with a covered wall-walk. Before the wall is an outer courtyard 15–17 m wide which was protected by a second wall and enclosed by a dry moat. The wall was defended with some 100 towers at intervals of one arrow-shot and was never taken by storm. In the 16th century it was reinforced again to protect it against the new firearms. These new bastions determine the present aspect of the town, which is dominated in particular by the sturdy round towers strategically positioned on the gates: the Laufer Torturm (1556), the Spittler Torturm (1557), the Frauentor (1558) and Neutor (1559). The castle, which was again reinforced in the 16th century, consists of two parts, the imperial castle and the burgrave's tower which still contains remains of the old Salic castle destroyed by Duke Henry of Bavaria in 1130: the pentagonal tower is the watchtower of Bergfried of that earlier castle. Conrad III, the first king of the Hohenstaufen dynasty, had a new castle built and had the old one rebuilt to be used as the seat of the burgraves. There was of course friction between the town and the burgraves, especially after 1313 when the town obtained responsibility for the imperial castle whenever the king was not in residence. Clashes occurred and the town felt itself obliged to build a defensive wall in front of the burgrave's castle and the Lungisland tower which dominated it. In 1388/89 the Nurembergers actually burnt down this castle and 30 years later it was destroyed again, this time by the Duke of Palatinate-Bavaria, whereupon the last burgrave Frederick VI of Hohenzollern sold it to Nuremberg together with the burgrave's rights. In 1494 he built the imperial stables (formerly a grain store) between the pentagonal tower and the Luginsland tower; it forms a good architectural counterweight to the hall-range of the imperial castle.

As the Hohenstaufen kings had once done, so too the high nobility now founded new towns. The Guelf Henry the Lion, the counterpart of the Hohenstaufen Frederick Barbarossa, founded Lübeck, Brunswick, Schwerin, Stade and Munich in Bavaria.

The history of the founding of Lübeck in the 12th century is related by Helmold in his 'Chronicle of the Slavs': 'Adolf, Count of Holstein, began to rebuild the castle of Segeberg and surrounded it with a wall. But since the land was empty of people, he sent messengers to all the countries, to Flanders, Holland, Utrecht, Westphalia and Friesland, and invited all those who had no land to come with their families; they would receive good, extensive and fertile land which would produce meat and fish in abundance and had excellent grazing . . . A great host of varied peoples responded to this call and set off with their families and their possessions and came to the land of the Wagrians . . . Then Count Adolf came to a place called Bucu where he found the walls of a deserted castle formerly built by Cruto, the enemy of God, and a very large island enclosed by two rivers: on one side flows the Trave, on the other the Wakenitz, both with marshy banks difficult of access. But on the land side a fairly narrow mound rises in front of the wall. Clearly recognizing how useful this site was and how excellent the harbour, the count began to build a town which he called Lübeck because it was situated not far from the old port and town of the same name which the [Slavic] prince Henry had once built.'

In 1157 the town was destroyed by fire. In the disputes between Count Adolf of Holstein and Duke Henry the Lion who had temporarily deprived the town of its market rights the duke finally acquired Lübeck after a new settlement founded by the count at a different spot had proved unsuccessful. At the command of the duke the merchants immediately returned there and abandoned the uncomfortable new town and began to rebuild the church and city walls. The duke sent messengers to the northern states, to Denmark, Sweden, Norway and Russia, offering them peace and freedom of access and passage through his town of Lübeck. He founded a mint and a customs house there and granted the town the most important privileges. Henceforth the commercial activity of the town increased constantly and the number of inhabitants rose greatly.'

More than a hundred years later Emperor Frederick II made Lübeck 'Reichsunmittelbar', i.e., subject to the emperor alone. In the charter of 1226 the emperor declared that Lübeck was an imperial city, that is directly subject to the emperor and independent of the territorial power of the princely or episcopal lords. The imperial cities were entitled to exercize the former princely privileges in their territory: administration, law, police, army, etc. Moreover they could take part in the imperial diets. The document states: 'In the name of the holy and indivisible Trinity Frederick II, Roman Emperor by the grace of God, perpetual enlarger of the Empire, King of Jerusalem and Sicily. Whenever the imperial majesty stretches out the hand of its generosity towards its subjects and faithful servants and rewards their merit with gifts of suitable compensation, it reinforces them in their persistent, pure loyalty and binds their will and that of the other faithful servants even more firmly in bonds of obedience to it. That is why, and We wish this to be made known to all present and future faithful servants of the empire – keeping before Our eyes the pure faith and genuine humility which all burgesses of Lübeck, our faithful servants, so laudably show towards us – in view of the important and welcome services which they have always tried so faithfully to perform for Us and the Empire, and which they will be able to perform for Us even better in the future . . . We desire to state firmly that the above-mentioned town shall always be free, i.e. shall be a free town, an imperial place directly subject to the imperial rule, and that it shall never be withdrawn from this direct rule; furthermore We decree that whenever a bailiff is appointed by the Empire to rule this town, only a man from the environs and borders of this town may be appointed to that office and that this bailiff shall also command the castle called Travemünde. Furthermore, in the desire to enlarge and expand the territory of the town under Our happy rule, We hereby add the following land and henceforth grant it to the town: from Padeluche brook to the Trave and from Padeluche brook upstream, along the border drawn there, as far as Crempelstorpe brook, then to the Drögen outwork and thence to the Trave. We also grant to the above-mentioned burgesses that no duty may be levied of any of their people in Oldesloe. In addition We grant that in the town they may make and mint a coint with Our Name which shall be valid for the duration of Our life and that of Henry, the illustrious Roman King, our

92

91–93 *Rothenburg on the Tauber. First mentioned as a castle in 804, the seat of the counts of Rothenburg until 1108 and an imperial town from 1172, in the 14th century Rothenburg commanded an area of 350 km² including 187 villages and 2 castles. This ancient imperial town still gives a good picture of a medieval German town although it was heavily bombed in 1945 when 306 houses, the town hall (except for the façade), 9 towers and 820 yards of the city wall were destroyed by incendiary and explosive bombs. Ill. 91 shows the 'Kobolzeller Gate', with the arms of the imperial town above the entrance. The city wall was built in 1350–1380 (Ill. 92).*

greatly beloved son; and for this they shall pay Our court sixty marks of silver each year. But if a new successor come to the throne in the future, then the coin shall be renewed for the same payment and with the same right and be valid during his lifetime; in that way, We decree, the coin shall pass from successor to successor as described above. Moreover We decree and grant that neither We nor any of Our imperial successors may demand hostages of them; instead the simple oath of loyalty towards the Empire will suffice and be taken as trust. Furthermore, all faithful merchants who come to the town over land or by water for their business shall come unharmed and depart

167

94 *Rothenburg on the Tauber. The outer gate of the hospital bastion dating from 1586. The bastion, planned in the form of a figure of eight, had a wall-walk so wide that artillery could be moved along it.*

without danger so long as they pay the relevant fee for which they are liable. In addition, We exempt the above-mentioned burgesses of Lübeck, when they travel to England, from the much misused and oppressive duty which the people of Cologne and Tiel and their companions have allegedly hatched up against them. Instead they shall live according to their birthright and standing like the people of Cologne and Tiel and their companions. We also confer on them the island opposite the castle of Travemünde called Priwolc for their future property according to municipal law as municipal territory. Furthermore We wish and decree that great care be taken so that no higher or lesser priest or laic should ever presume to build a fortification or a castle on the Trave upriver from the town as far as the source, downriver from the town to the sea or on either bank for two miles; and We strictly prohibit any outside bailiff from presuming to exercize his stewardship within the town limits or to legislate. And because in future We wish to protect the burgesses from all heavy and undue levies, We strictly forbid that the tax called 'Ungelt' be levied of them or required of them anywhere in the whole county of Saxony. Moreover, no prince, lord or noblemen from bordering areas shall presume to prevent any subsistence goods from being bought into the town of Lübeck from elsewhere, whether from Hamburg, from Ratzeburg, from Wittenburg, from Schwerin or from the whole of the country of Borwin and his son; and every Lübeck burgess, whether rich or poor, may buy or sell without impediment in all these lands. And We strictly forbid it that any greater or lesser clergyman or laic give any person safe conduct into this town so that this person need not account for himself before the court if summoned. Moreover We wish and emphatically command that if and when any of these burgesses is shipwrecked anywhere in the Empire, any goods that he has managed to salvage from this peril be left to him without hindrance or argument. We also grant them the landed property outside Travemünde, beside the port, by the harbour sign; and We give them permission freely to use the land to the benefit of the town of Lübeck. In the fullness of Our grace We grant and confirm in perpetuity their rights, together with all the good usages and customs, which they have been proven to possess since the time of the late Emperor Frederick, our grandfather of blessed memory. At the same time We lay down and by virtue of this document expressly decree that no lesser or greater clergyman or laic shall dare wantonly to hinder or harass the above-mentioned burgesses of Lübeck, Our faithful servants, in any of the above. Let anyone who dares to do so know that in punishment for his crime he shall be liable to Our disfavour and the fine of five hundred pounds in pure gold, half of which shall be paid into Our treasury, the other half to those who have suffered the injury. To ensure that all this shall ever remain legal and inviolable, We have had this document drawn up and endorsed with the wax seal of Our Majesty.'

Berthold III of Zähringen founded Freiburg on the model of Cologne and adopted the same charter of liberties. Here too settlers were attracted by the offer of free building sites; again they were largely exempted from duties in the ducal district and could elect the mayor and parson. Many towns were also founded in Switzerland on this model, including Freiburg Im Uchtland (1157) and Bern (1191).

As we have said, the royal towns were situated on crown land and were thus directly subject to the king. If they managed to gain exemption from the tax ('Bede') to be paid to the king, they were called free imperial cities. These imperial cities were very concerned lest the king sell or mortgage his sovereign rights over the town since if the pledge was not redeemed, they would fall into the power of the mortgagee and simply become country towns. Often their only recourse was to redeem the pledge themselves.

In order to avoid any such sale or mortgaging and in order to consolidate

Pages 173–176:
95–98 Rothenburg on the Tauber. Inner hospital gate (Ill. 95): View from the so-called 'Plönlein' tower towards the market place (Ill. 96); view from the town hall tower to the castle gate (Ill. 97); view from the town hall tower over the town to the east. In the background one can see the city wall with its wall-walk and the Outer 'Röder' Gate (right) and the Würzburger Gate (Ill. 98). The medieval town of Rothenburg was rediscovered with great enthusiasm by the 19th-century Romantic painters.

LÖWEN-APOTHEKE

their political influence, for instance at the imperial diets where they usually had equal rights with the princes, the imperial cities associated themselves on the model of the northern Italian federations. The Swabian city league (Ulm, Constance, Lindau, St Gall, Ravensburg, Reutlinger and others) was founded in 1376 and the Rhenish league (Colmar, Strasbourg, Mühlhausen, Speyer, Worms, Frankfurt, etc.) in 1381. Eventually the two fused into the South German League. Occasionally even princes joined the city leagues if this seemed in their political interests. Yet the driving force behind this movement was the intention of the towns to resist the arbitrary power of emperor or princes and to obtain greater independence, unlike the Hanseatic league of cities round the Baltic Sea which had been founded in the 13th century purely for economic reasons (protection of the merchants, security of trade relations and markets). In 1385 the South German League allied itself with a part of the Swiss Confederation (Bern, Zürich, Zug, Lucerne). The Swiss confederates had to act alone in their disputes with the Habsburgers, however they managed completely to defeat the Austrian knights at the Battles of Sempach (1368) and Nafels (1388), which led to the independence of Switzerland from the Habsburg territorial state in 1389. The German city leagues were less fortunate; in 1388 the Swabian towns were beaten by Count Eberhard of Württemberg at Döffingen and in the same year the Rhenish towns were defeated by Count Ruprecht of the Palatinate. The following year King Wenceslas dissolved the leagues and in spite of renowned attempts to ally themselves the German towns were never to recover from this defeat.

Three examples of very well-preserved medieval towns are Rothenburg ob der Tauber, Dinkelsbühl and Nordlingen.

Rothenburg ob der Tauber (Ills. 91–98) grew up beside the county castle of the same name on the narrow spur of a hill round which flowed the Tauber river. Today all that remains is the former castle chapel, for the castle itself was destroyed by an earthquake in 1356 and Emperor Charles IV decided not to have it rebuilt but left it to the town. A flourishing town soon grew up on the site of the castle which allegedly obtained imperial privileges as early as 1172 and became a free imperial city in 1274. It experienced a great economic expansion in the 14th century, which produced increased building activity. Rothenburg belonged to a league and was besieged for weeks during the inter-city wars. In 1525, a year after joining the Reformation movement, it took part in the Peasant War in which the peasants suffered a bloody defeat. During the Thirty Years War it therefore supported the Protestant Union. It was besieged and conquered in 1631 by the commander-in-chief of the Catholic League, Tilly. After the Thirty Years War the economic situation gradually worsened until the town was rediscovered for tourism. The medieval Rothenburg spread along the main road, the so-called Herrngasse, which divides the town in two halves. From the south a second main road leads to the central market place where all the axis roads meet. The town was expanded several times, but even today the town plan clearly shows the limits of the earliest town. The incomparably beautiful town is characterized by a strong defensive system (city wall and gates) the picturesque house fronts along the narrow streets, most of which run in straight lines, and the proud and impressive buildings enclosing the market-place, including the splendid town hall which is one of the most beautiful in Germany.

Dinkelsbühl (Ills. 99–101) is situated on Wörnitzfurt river and lies at the intersection of old north-south and west-east axis roads. The town, owned by the Hohenstaufen, had already achieved a certain importance in the 12th century. But in 1251 it was mortgaged to the counts of Öttingen together with Nördlingen and Harburg. In 1305 it obtained the same civic liberties as Ulm under an imperial charter, but it was not able to buy its freedom from the counts until the mid-century. From 1351 it was an imperial city and was ruled

by a twenty-four-man town council made up of patricians and representatives of the guilds. In 1541 Dingelsbühl joined the Augsburg Confession, the first Protestant creed, drawn up by Philip Melanchthon. But after the intervention of the emperor in 1552 the city was ruled by a Catholic minority until the Peace of Westphalia in 1648. Dinkelsbühl has no real market place but like many of the Hohenstaufen cities it has wide market streets flanked by stately town houses. The city wall with wall-walk and many towers still encircles the town completely. Four gates open to the four points of the compass: the Wörnitztor and the Nördlinger (Ill. 101), Segringer and Rothenburger gates. They corresponded to the four roads which intersected in Dinkelsbühl and determined the layout and spread of the town which still forms a well-planned and clear whole today.

Nördlingen (Ills. 102–104) stands on the site of an ancient Roman settlement. There is evidence of a later Alemannic settlement too which came under the bishop of Regensburg in 898. Subsequently Nördlingen became an important market town because of its useful commercial position and in 1215 it came into the hands of Emperor Frederick II under an exchange. A fair is mentioned in Nördlingen as early as 1219; it was the largest in northern Germany after that of Frankfurt, trading mainly in clothes and furs. The city was granted privileges by Louis of Bavaria and Charles IV and these laid the foundation of its later status of free imperial city. The plan of the town forms an almost regular circle and the various circles of growth are still clearly apparent. The oldest nucleus of the town is the harbour market area, the meeting place of the old major roads from Ulm, Munich and the Rems valley. A fortification wall is first mentioned in 1243. In 1327 the suburbs which had already developed were incorporated inside a new city wall, thus halting any

102 Nördlingen. The 'Löpsinger' Gate dating from 1592.

Nördlingen, engraving by Andreas Zeidler, 1651

further expansion. This wall (Ill. 103) is astonishingly well-preserved and was reinforced with bastions in the 16th century; the gates also date from the 14th to 17th centuries.

Although the German tribes were clearly anti-urban when they penetrated into Roman territory, the town began to increase in importance in medieval Europe, and in particular in Germany. In 900 there were some forty towns in Germany, in 1200 there were two hundred and fifty. In the 13th century alone at least 800 German towns were founded and towards the end of the Middle

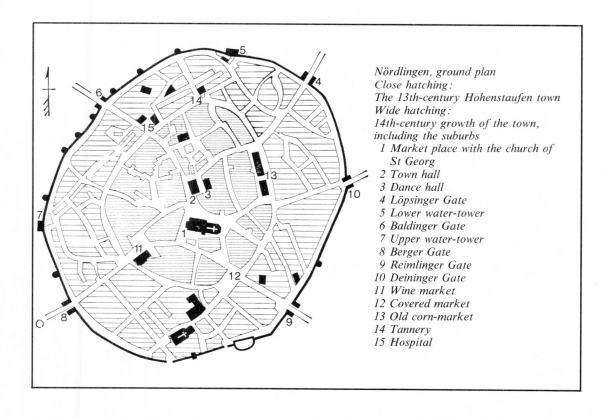

Nördlingen, ground plan
Close hatching:
The 13th-century Hohenstaufen town
Wide hatching:
14th-century growth of the town,
including the suburbs
  1 *Market place with the church of*
    St Georg
  2 *Town hall*
  3 *Dance hall*
  4 *Löpsinger Gate*
  5 *Lower water-tower*
  6 *Baldinger Gate*
  7 *Upper water-tower*
  8 *Berger Gate*
  9 *Reimlinger Gate*
10 *Deininger Gate*
11 *Wine market*
12 *Covered market*
13 *Old corn-market*
14 *Tannery*
15 *Hospital*

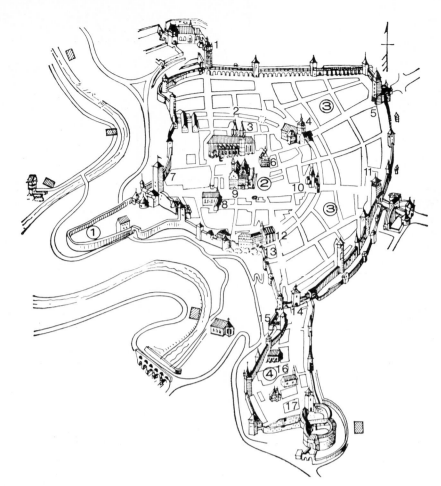

Rothenburg on the Tauber
① *Site of the original castle*
② *12th-century Hohenstaufen town*
③ *13th-century growth of the town*
④ *Late 14th-century incorporation of the*
   southern suburb with the hospital
 1 *Klingen Gate*
 2 *(former) Blue Gatehouse*
 3 *Church of St Jacob*
 4 *White Gatehouse*
 5 *Würzburger Gate*
 6 *Town-hall cellar-restaurant*
 7 *Castle gate*
 8 *(former) Church of St Francis*
 9 *Market, town hall*
10 *Inner Röder Gate*
11 *Outer Röder Gate*
12 *Church of St John*
13 *(former) Gate of St John*
14 *Inner hospital gate (Siebers tower)*
15 *Kobolzeller Gate*
16 *Hospital church*
17 *Outer hospital gate*

Ages the figure was some 3000 towns with charters of liberties, so that at that time every third or fourth German was a townsman.

As regards size and population, compared to our modern towns the medieval town was relatively small and often had no more than 1000 inhabitants. Towns with a population of about 10,000 were considered large towns. In *c.* 1400 the largest German town, Cologne, had 40,000 inhabitants; the largest towns in Europe as a whole were Venice, Milan, London and Paris where the figure sometimes reached 100,000 or more. By comparison, the Arab town of Cordoba in Spain already numbered about 1 million inhabitants in the 10th century.

With the growth of the towns from the 13th century onwards, economic, intellectual and cultural life was concentrated increasingly in the town and urban civilization took the place of the former aristocratic and rural way of life.

Medieval Urban Culture: Schools and Universities

As we have noted, the medieval towns were relatively small. This makes their cultural achievements all the more surprising. These towns became centres of artistic activity and the site of the first lay schools and universities.

After the collapse of the civilization of Antiquity, the Christian monasteries slowly became the major cultural centres. According to the rules of the Benedictine Order, monks had to spend four hours a day studying the Holy Scriptures and in choral song. Magnificent manuscripts were created in these monasteries, many of them illuminated: poetry, history, copies of the Greek and Roman classics, etc. The monasteries also set up their own monastery schools; the first ones in German-speaking countries were founded in the 7th century. The most famous of the German monastery schools were Fulda,

Korvei, Hirsau, Reichenau, Hersfeld and St Gall. Soon these schools were opened to people other than monks. The monasteries also founded the first primary schools. The biographer of Abbot William of Dijon who founded schools for 'ignorant' laics at the beginning of the 11th century wrote: 'Since he wanted to combat this ignorance, he founded primary schools in the monasteries of Normandy and in all other regions of France, where talented teachers were to instruct all who lived there; rich or poor, they all had equally free access. Those without funds were even kept at the monastery's cost.' On the model of the monastery schools, cathedral schools were frequently founded in episcopal churches where the priests were also trained. But for a long time the great majority of laics, including the nobility, remained illiterate. There was no real change in this situation until the period of flowering of the towns. Trade and the increasing autonomy of the towns called for a new and better training of the merchants and burgesses. In line with the historical development of the towns which was now based on economic factors, the first urban schools were set up in Italian towns. These schools of arithmetic and writing instructed children in reading, writing, arithmetic and Latin. This schooling also spread north of the Alps in the 12th century.

The rudimentary education and training which had grown up in response to the needs of the time was further stimulated by the influence of the superior culture of the Byzantines and Arabs and through their intermediary by the rediscovery of Greek and Roman Antiquity. So once again Arab scholarship and Antiquity exerted a decisive influence on urban culture. The English scholastic philosopher Adelard of Bath (d. *c.* 1160) who travelled through Spain, Italy and the Near East described the new attitude of the scholar to experience and logic: 'I have learned from my Arab teachers to take common sense as my guide; you, however, are content slavishly to follow a chain of fabulous authorities. What other name can one give to authority than that of a chain? To be led by a chain like the unreasonable animals and not to know where or why – they are led and they are content to follow the cord that leads them – and so most of you are captives in an animal-like credulity and let yourselves be seduced blindly to dangerous opinions by the authority of what is written.' The new, enlightened spirit which grew out of the encounter with other cultures and soon led to doubts regarding the firm order of God, Church and King or Emperor is also illustrated by an excerpt from the work of William of Conches (1080–1154), the French grammarian and philosopher and the main representative of the School of Chartres: 'What is important is not that God could do all this, but to examine it and to explain it rationally, to show its purpose and use. Certainly, God can do everything. What is important, however, is that He did this or that. God can make a tree trunk into a calf, as the peasants say. But has He ever done so?'

A medical college was probably founded in Salerno as early as the 9th century. The founders were a Greek, a Latin, a Jew and an Arab. At that time southern Italy and Sicily were still under Arab influence (Arab occupation of Traetto on the Garigliano river and of Agropoli south of Phaestum/Salerno in 800). For a long time the doctors of Salerno were the most famous in Europe. William the Conqueror was treated there for a war wound, and after the First Crusade Count Robert of Normandy who had been wounded near Jerusalem and his knights also sought treatment there. In the 11th century Montpellier became famous as the seat of medical science; there has been a faculty of medicine there since 1220 which was supplemented in 1230 by a faculty of law. We may presume that Arab medical knowledge had penetrated here too, to the south-western border area with Arabic Spain.

When Europe fell victim to the plague, the Black Death (1348–1352), which killed almost one-third of the population, the Andalusian statesman and

103 *Nördlingen. First mentioned in 898 as crown domain, Nördlingen later became the property of St Emmeran in Regensburg for a time. From c. 1215 until 1805 it was a free imperial town. The appearance of the town has remained almost unchanged through the ages.*

184

doctor Ibn al-Chatib (1313–1374) wrote: 'The existence of the infection is established by experience, research and the evidence of the senses, autopsy and authentic evidence: these facts give the irrefutable proof. The fact of the infection is verified by the researcher who notes that a person who comes into contact with persons suffering from the disease also falls sick, whereas he who has not come into contact with them remains unaffected; furthermore that the disease can be transmitted in a house or area by a dress or a vessel so that even an earring can mean death for the person who puts it on and can then bring the whole house into ruin; furthermore that it can appear in a single house in a town and then flare up among those who have had some dealing with the sick person, then among the neighbours and all those who have visited the house of the sick person . . . furthermore it has been proved that the infection can spread from someone who has arrived from an infected country at a port and that persons in quarantine are immune.' This realization of the infectiousness of diseases and plagues was one of the most important medical advances of a time when Christian Europe was still holding the Jews responsible for the plague and persecuted them mercilessly, as Tilemann Ehlen of Wolfhagen graphically describes in the famous 'Limburg Chronicle': 'In the year 1349 a great death came over the German lands, what is called the first great death. The people died of the glands, and anyone who was affected usually died on the third day. And the people died in the great towns of Mainz, Cologne and so on, usually more than a hundred of them every day . . . In this jubilee year, when the dying ended, the Jews were generally killed and burned in the German lands. This was done by the princes, counts, lords and towns, excepting the Duke of Austria who protected his Jews. The Jews were accused of having poisoned the Christians because so many of these had died.' But when Europe was visited by the second epidemic of plague, people had become a little more intelligent – at least in Montpellier where Chalin de Vinario, professor at the University, admitted only one reason for the furious spread of the plague in 1382: '. . . that the disease cannot be transmitted from any other cause or any other source than infection.' The two schools of Salerno and Montpellier occupy a special position among the early universities because they were not run by the clergy, that is to say they had not developed out of cathedral schools. This trend became increasingly common after the end of the 12th century and the cathedral schools correspondingly dwindled in less importance after 1150.

The new type of university was called 'Studium generale' as opposed to the 'Studia particularia' of the various church schools. The new universities were open to all, so that the term 'Studium generale' refers not to the number of subjects studied but to the fact that all students were admitted. The term 'university' was not adopted until later and originally meant a corporation of all teachers ('Universitas scolarium') and all students ('Universitas scolarium'). In 1219 Paris University was thus called 'Universitas magistrorum et scolarium Parisiensium'.

In general one can distinguish between two main types of medieval university: the clerical, masters' university of the north, mainly represented by Paris, and the students' university of the south, whose teaching staff was made up of laymen and for which the prototype was the University of Bologna. The University of Paris, founded in the 12th century, was given the honorary title of 'Mother of the sciences' and became the model for almost all the other European universities. In 1231 it was withdrawn from the sphere of jurisdiction of the bishop of Paris and became fully self-governing, subject only to the authority of the pope. It had three higher faculties; theology, canon law and medicine; another one, the so-called faculty of arts, was the obligatory preparation for the higher faculties. The faculty of arts gave instruction in the seven liberal arts ('artes liberales') of grammar, rhetoric,

104 *Nördlingen. The city wall with its picturesque wall-walk and 16 defensive towers dates from the 14th century and now encloses the city centre.*

dialectic, astronomy, arithmetic, geometry and music.

In Bologna it was law that flourished. Unlike in Paris, the teachers here depended on the fees paid by the students, which gave the students great influence over the administration. Throughout Europe the precondition for attending a university was mastery of Latin, the only teaching language; there was no preparatory school so that even twelve- and thirteen-year-olds could attend the university. Some 4000 to 5000 students studied at the University of Paris in the 13th century. In general a far greater number of people were academically educated then than now. There were even students' hostels ('collegia') for poor students. In 1258 the court chaplain of St Louis, Robert de Sorbon, endowed a hostel for poor students and teachers of theology; his name was later used as the title of the whole university (Sorbonne).

As a rule the universities were endowed by popes and emperors. In 1347 Emperor Charles IV founded the first university on German soil, the University of Prague. The letter of endowment states: 'In order that our Kingdom of Bohemia, which has an excess of worldly goods having been blessed by the grace of God with a fertile soil, should also through our care and organization be adorned with an abundance of perceptive men, so that our faithful subjects who are for ever hungry for the fruit of knowledge shall find it spread before them in our country and find it superfluous to travel the globe in search of scholarship, to seek out strange people or to beg in other countries; rather shall they deem it laudable to bring in strangers . . .'

Here we already find the expression of a sense of nationalism which was to develop into the ideological equivalent of the national state following the more collective European spirit of the early and late Middle Ages.

With the emergence of the numerous universities in the 13th and 14th centuries, European urban culture took on its definitive form as a secular and profane culture, committed to an undogmatic search for truth and progressive by nature. Scientific method was gradually established and it seemed that this would lead to man's coming of age, that the individual could free himself from the strict world order the visible expression of which had been social (feudal) relations. Now a freer spirit began to emerge, one which did not remain silent in public – to the annoyance of the representatives of the old order, as is shown by the words of the abbot of Sainte Geneviève in Paris, Stephen of Tournai: 'People debate openly and thus offend against the hallowed constitutions, the mystery of the divinity and the incarnation of the Word . . . The indivisible Trinity is hacked to pieces at street-corners. There are as many errors as doctors, as many scandals as auditoriums, as many blasphemies as public places.' The abbot's criticisms clearly betray his discomfort at the publicity of the towns. Without going in detail about the cultural achievements of the medieval towns, stress must be laid on one characteristic of urban culture compared to the select and aristocratic culture of the knights, since it opened the way to the further social and cultural development of Europe. That is the greater publicity created by the towns and condemned by Stephen of Tournai. Even the architectural framework of the two different social orders reflects the differences. The remote and almost inaccessible castles were military bases but also represented the social and cultural centres of the feudal age. The lord lived here in seclusion with his family. Minstrels, players and troubadours appeared before the small circle of castle society, travelling from castle to castle. They were not very numerous, but in the castles any change from the monotonous life was celebrated to the full. In the towns, by contrast, there was a press of people, and an animated life inhabited the narrow alleyways and large and small squares between splendid churches and imposing town halls, emporiums and stores, halls of commerce, butchers' stalls and the more modest private houses which were still built of wood, lime and straw until the beginning of the 13th century. The towns, which were usually situated at the intersection of trade routes, were meeting-places for merchants and travellers from the most distant lands who brought not only their wares but news and tales of unknown lands and peoples, strange customs, new inventions, technical improvements, artistic achievements and scientific discoveries. All this was greedily absorbed and discussed in the towns. Even the great reversals caused by famine and epidemics (Bubonic Plague) in the 14th century which threw the European economy into a major crisis and decimated the population of Europe from some 73 to only 45 million inhabitants could not halt the development in the towns of a bourgeois civilization open to the world. On the threshold of modern times, which can be marked summarily by the discovery of America in 1492 – which shattered the existing geographical boundaries – and the Reformation (Luther's theses, 1517) – which shattered the medieval view of the world – a report dating from 1490 describes the town of Vienna as follows: 'The town is situated in a half moon on the Danube, the city wall is a good 5000 steps long and has double walls. The actual town lies like a palace in the middle of its suburbs, several of which rival it in beauty and size. Every habitation has something worth seeing, worth considering. Almost every house has its back yard and its forecourt, extensive halls and also good winter rooms. The guest rooms are very beautifully panelled, magnificently appointed and have fires. There is glass in all the windows, much of it beautifully painted, and protected against thieves by iron bars. Below the ground are extensive wine cellars and vaults; there are used for pharmacies, storage, general stores and rented accommodation for strangers and natives. In the halls and summer rooms there are so many birds that anyone passing through the street might think himself in the middle of a delightful green wood. Great activity reigns on the streets and in the market places. Before the last war 50,000 souls and 7,000 students were counted, not including children and adolescents. There is a vast confluence of merchants and masses of money is earned. The whole area of Vienna is but a large, splendid garden, crowned with lovely vineyards and orchards, adorned with the most charming country houses.' The urban prosperity and the new living conditions also led, however, to a decline in morals, which emerges from the same description: 'Day and night there are great battles in the streets, the artisans take arms against the students, the courtiers against the burgesses, the burgesses against each other. It is rare for a church celebration to end without bloody quarrels and murder and assassination are frequent. Nearly every burgess keeps winehouses and taverns to which they summon drinking companions and 'easy' women. The people are devoted only to the body and on Sunday they dissipate what they have earned in the week. The number of open prostitutes is very large and few women are content with just *one* man. Often noblemen visit beautiful bourgeois women. Then the husband brings wine to serve the elegant guest whereupon he leaves him alone with his wife. The rich old merchants take young maids in marriage and as soon as these maids have become widows they marry their house boys with whom they have long been committing adultery. It is also said that many women get rid of their troublesome husbands with poison and it is certain that burghers who will not tolerate the immoral intercourse of their wife and daughters with young courtiers are often assassinated while these go free.' The situation must have been similar in all the European towns of that time. But probably this is not the reverse side of the same medal as has often been asserted, but rather the inevitable crisis of a society released from the firm bonds of the medieval world which had to find its way to a new understanding of itself and a new social order. New, binding values applicable to the individual and to society as a whole emerged with the advent of humanism and the Reformation both of which had been heralded by the urban culture of the Middle Ages and now ushered in a new period of history.

189